The Psychoanalysis of Organizations

A psychoanalytic approach
to behaviour in groups
and organizations.

n.b.   p 76-77 -   T. groups.

To Mary, Nicholas, and Louise

Robert de Board

The Psychoanalysis of Organizations

A psychoanalytic approach
to behaviour in groups
and organizations

Tavistock/Routledge
London and New York

First published in 1978 by Tavistock Publications Limited
Reprinted in 1990 and 1991 by Routledge
11 New Fetter Lane, London EC4P 4EE

Simultaneously published in the USA and Canada
by Routledge
a division of Routledge, Chapman and Hall, Inc.
29 West 35th Street, New York, NY 10001

Typeset by Red Lion Setters, Holborn, London
Printed in Great Britain at
the University Printing House, Cambridge

ISBN 0-415-05175-4

Contents

Acknowledgements

The author and publishers are grateful to the various individuals and publishers who have given permission for material to be reproduced.

Figure 1 on page 8 is reprinted from *Readings in Social Psychology* (1966: 236, 237), edited by E. Maccoby, T. Newcomb and E. Hartley, with permission of the publishers, Methuen & Co. *Figure 2* on page 19 is printed from *Group Psychology and the Analysis of the Ego* (1922: 80) by S. Freud, by permission of the publishers, International Psycho-analytic Press. *Figure 4* on page 52 is reprinted from 'Frontiers in Group Dynamics' (1947) by K. Lewin, from *Human Relations 1*(1): 11. *Figure 5* on page 56 is reprinted from 'Need Force and Valence in Psychological Fields' (1972: 203) by K. Lewin, in *Classic Contributions to Social Psychology*, edited by E.P. Hollander and R.G. Hunt, by permission of Oxford University Press. *Figure 6* on page 57 is reprinted from 'Regression, Retrogression, and Development' (1952: 92). by K. Lewin, from *Field Theory in Social Science*, edited by D. Cartwright, by permission of Tavistock Publications. *Figure 7* on page 67 is reprinted from *Improving Skills in Working with People: the T-Group* (1969: 2) by P.B. Smith, with the permission of Her Majesty's Stationery Office. *Figure 8* on page 90 is reprinted from 'Individual Groups and Intergroup Processes' (1969: 575) by A.K. Rice, from *Human Relations 22*(6): 575. *Figure 10* on page 100 is reprinted from *Productivity and Social Organization* (1958: 60) by A.K. Rice, with the permission of Tavistock Publications. *Figure 11* on page 128 is reprinted from *A Life Apart* (1972: 190) by E. Miller and G. Gwynne with the permission of Tavistock Publications.

Introduction

This book is the result of my attempt to try and understand what happens to people who work in groups and organizations. I have spent over twenty years working in a variety of organizations, which have included a chemical company, the army (though not from choice), the Church of England, a motor manufacturing company, and now an academic institution. While their differences are far greater than their similarities, each of these organizations has had the same ability to affect my happiness in a profound way. If, for example, I completed a project successfully and enjoyed the company of my fellow workers, then the whole of my life seemed enlarged, happy, and worthwhile. At other times, undemanding work, authoritarian bosses, and hostile rivalry seemed to reduce my life to a prison and in two instances I resigned from the organization.

One common effect all organizations seem able to produce is the promotion of non-human objectives above people, so that the human spirit is sacrificed to such sterile aims as profit and technology. One answer is to retire to the hills, grow organic foods, and live in a house powered by wind and sun. However, I would argue that modern society is too complex and too interdependent to develop in this way. The answer, perhaps, lies in developing organizations that produce wealth and which *at the same time*, enable the people working in them to maintain and develop their humanity. How this will happen is uncertain. It poses many political questions concerning power, authority, and ownership and the current and growing concern about participation is one example of this. It also includes the problem of the allocation of the nation's resources such as the amount of welfare and social services that a country should provide from its total revenue.

But in terms of organization, all this, leads to the concept of 'choice' and to the growing realization that the primary objectives of an organization must be human objectives; money and technology are simply the ways of achieving this. At the moment, in spite of economic hardships, many people, especially young graduates, exercise their choice by joining organizations which, apparently, have a greater concern with people than technology. The social services and education, especially further education, have never been so enlarged, while for instance, the engineering industry is failing to attract and retain graduates.

If a country is to generate wealth then the choice should not be one of opting out of the 'hard-line' manufacturing industries, but rather of organizing such industries in ways which satisfy the innate humanity of each person who works in them. And of course, organizations that are primarily devoted to people, such as the social services, can themselves exhibit all the dehumanizing aspects of the worst sort of bureaucracy.

However, it seems to me unlikely that much progress will be made until there is a wider understanding of the way people behave. There are now so many books dealing with this area of 'organizational behaviour' that it is with some trepidation that I offer yet another. Nevertheless I do so, because I believe that some of the theories and evidence contained in this book offer genuine insights into what actually happens when people work together in groups and organizations.

In the last analysis, each person works for himself, unless some kind of pressure forces him in another direction. What psychoanalysis helps to reveal are those processes which occur within every individual and which determine how each person will act. It shows how psychological pressures, especially anxiety, can neutralize productive effort and drain away human energy. It shows the ways in which people affect and relate to each other in groups, and the ways in which leaders are created. Above all, I think, it shows some of the basic causes of problems which are likely to occur in any organization, but which are rarely understood, and therefore rarely solved, by managers.

In this book I have attempted to bring together theories and evidence from a variety of sources and show how they are interconnected. In the final chapter I have developed my own ideas in order to elucidate the particular relationship between psychoanalysis and the work carried out in groups and organizations.

In all cases I have tried to present theory and argument as clearly and as simply as possible.

I hope that this book will be found useful, not only by practical managers, but also by students of management and organization, and that it will make a contribution to one of the most urgent problems of today — how to make organizations fit for human beings.

R. de Board
Henley Staff College
September 1977

1 Early studies of group behaviour

A study of human behaviour in groups and organizations has its origins in many separate and distinct pieces of work. Certainly before the 1930s, this was not a generally recognized field of study and different countries produced a variety of people who, reflecting their own cultures and social climates, looked at groups and organizations from a number of different standpoints. This chapter gives a brief survey of this early work and then examines in more detail four contributions which can now be seen to be of particular importance.

A. *Max Weber* (1864-1920)

At Berlin University, with its strict formality and academic discipline, Max Weber studied the historical development of civilizations through the sociology of their religious and economic life. His book, *The Protestant Ethic and the Spirit of Capitalism* (Weber 1930), remains a classic study of the impact of Protestant beliefs on the development of capitalism in Western Europe and the United States. But he also made a major contribution to the study of organizations, classifying them as: 'charismatic', 'traditional', and 'rational-legal' depending on the way in which authority is used and legitimized within them. He analysed the bureaucratic type of organization in particular, and did not regard it as an inefficient, ponderous structure (as the word is usually understood today) but as a form of organization that technically is the most efficient system possible. Weber used the word 'bureaucracy' because central to this form of organization is a 'bureau' where all written records and files are stored for safe keeping. The work and ideas of Weber, and especially his categories of organizations, have greatly influenced the formal studies of organization structure.

B. *Kurt Lewin* (1890-1947)

Between 1924 and 1926, work of a very different nature was being carried out in the Psychological Institute of Weber's university at Berlin. A young psychologist, Kurt Lewin, was working with a small and enthusiastic team of scientists who were all influenced by the new ideas of 'Gestalt' psychology. Their empirical studies were concerned with the role of goal achievement in the release of tensions.* One particular study (by Bluma Zeigarnick) found that when people were interrupted in the middle of a task, they could remember the unfinished parts of the task at a later period much better than they could recall the parts they had completed. Lewin explained this by saying that there was a psychological 'tension' associated with the unfinished tasks which caused them to be recalled in preference to the finished tasks. As Chapter 6 will show, these ideas of psychological forces and tensions were to be developed by Lewin and would greatly influence the study of group dynamics.

C. *Sigmund Freud* (1856-1939)

The powerful and unique influence of Freud and his theories of psychoanalysis increasingly became known by the beginning of this century. The concept of the unconscious, as a factor affecting behaviour, and especially the centrality of sex in all human actions, was to affect every aspect of human psychology. Freud, although mainly concentrating on individual behaviour and the therapeutic affect of psychoanalysis, sought to extend the application of his ideas and theories to groups, organizations, and society. In 1912 he published *Totem and Taboo* in which he analysed anthropological material in terms of psychoanalytic theory. In the first human group, which he called the 'primal horde', the most significant action occurred when the group over-threw and killed the despotic leader and this generated the beginning of religion, morality, and social organization.

*Marrow (1969) gives a full description of the Berlin experiments.

In 1922 Freud published *Group Psychology and the Analysis of the Ego*, which attempted to explain the nature of the bonding in a group — what made a group into a group — and the role and influence of the leader. This book, which will be analysed in detail in Chapter 2, shows the breadth of Freud's thinking, including examples which range from a group of two to such large organizations as the army and the church.

D. *F.W. Taylor* (1856-1917)

Not all the thinking and writing about organizations and groups was being carried out by academics. In terms of influence, the work and writings of Frederick Winslow Taylor have had a profound and lasting effect on the management of organizations. Taylor developed what he called 'The Principles of Scientific Management' which was also the title of his book published in 1911. For Taylor: 'What the workmen want from their employers beyond anything else is high wages', and he believed that 'scientific management' could overcome any obstacle to the workmen achieving this. Underlying all Taylor's writings is the assumption that the desire to maximize earnings is the only motivating factor which induces man to work.

Taylor's ideas were always controversial. He was sacked from the Bethlehem Steel Company in 1901 and his methods were investigated by the United States Commission on Industrial Relations in 1914. Few, if any, managers would agree with Taylor's principles today, but many organizations reveal his influence through their continuing use of 'Work Study' methods.

E. *Henri Fayol* (1841-1925)

Fayol was a French mining engineer who was Managing Director of a large mining and metallurgical combine for thirty years. Drawing on his experience, he analysed the nature of organizations, especially the nature of management (Fayol 1949). He defined management as comprising five elements, which were: (a) to forecast and plan, (b) to organize, (c) to command, (d) to co-ordinate, and (e) to control. Fayol is the earliest known proponent of a theoretical analysis of managerial work and his five elements are still able to help managers clarify their thinking in an organization today.

These examples of Weber, Lewin, Freud, Taylor, and Fayol show some of the origins of work in the area of groups, organizations, and the way people behave in them. However, in the period between 1920 and 1939, four separate pieces of work were carried out, which, because of the empirical nature of the experiments, provided a foundation of fact which continues to be relevant to the present situation.

1 *Elton Mayo and the experiments at Hawthorne*

In 1924 a number of engineers carried out an enquiry at the Hawthorne plant of the Western Electric Company in the United States that studied the relationship between illumination and efficiency. These experiments involved varying the intensity of the electric lighting and measuring the effect this had on the output of groups of workers. Control groups were used, where no changes in lighting were made, and their output was compared with that of the experimental groups. The results were odd and inconclusive. Quoting from the original report: 'The output bobbed up and down without direct relation to the amount of illumination' (Roethlisberger and Dickson 1946: 15). It also produced very appreciable and almost identical production increases in both the control and test groups. But although the results were inconclusive they contributed to the steadily growing realization that more knowledge concerning problems involving human factors was essential.

At this point, Mayo took over the enquiry and brought in the Industrial Research team from Harvard University, where he was Professor of Industrial Research. His original enquiry sought to answer six questions:

(a) Do employees actually get tired out?
(b) Are rest pauses desirable?
(c) Is a shorter working day possible?
(d) What are the attitudes of employees towards their work and towards the company?
(e) What is the effect of changing the type of working equipment?
(f) Why does production fall off in the afternoon?

The first stage of Mayo's work commenced in 1927 and is

known as the 'Relay Assembly Test Room' experiment. In this experiment six female operators, aged between nineteen and twenty-nine (average age twenty-two) were put into a room in which each individual's output of assembled telephone relays could be measured. For a period of just over two years, from April 1927 to June 1929, this group worked together in a variety of planned 'changed' situations, designed to discover the effect of fatigue on performance.*

During the two years, thirteen changes were made concerning frequency of rest pauses, length of working hours, and the nature of wage incentives, each change lasting from four to twelve weeks, excepting the final period, which lasted for thirty-one weeks. The results made history. Significant increases in production were obtained progressively in periods that had nominally the same working conditions. Most surprisingly, output continued to increase even when the working conditions reverted to the original situation of a long working day without rest pauses. Mayo explains it in this way:

'What actually happened was that six individuals became a team and the team gave itself whole-heartedly and spontaneously to co-operation in the experiment. The consequence was that they felt themselves to be participating freely and without afterthought, and were happy in the knowledge that they were working without coercion from above or limitation from below.' (Mayo 1945: 72)

The results of this research led Mayo to place major emphasis on the social organization of the work group and the informal standards governing the behaviour of the work group members. This latter point emerged again in the 'Bank Wiring Room' experiment, where fourteen men were selected to work together on wiring and soldering banks of telephone terminals. For approximately eighteen months, from 1930 to 1932, an observer sat in with them and observed their working behaviour. One of the facts which emerged was that the group, although on an incentive bonus, restricted its output to its own agreed level.

*Two workers were expelled from the group after eight months for behaviour 'approaching gross insubordination' and replaced by two others (Roethlisberger and Dickson 1946: 54)

Strong group pressures ensured that individuals were aware of breaking these group norms, either by acting as 'rate-busters' or as 'chiselers'.

Mayo's work has not been without its critics, who have concentrated, probably fairly, on its bias towards management, and the exaltation of empiricism and observation, and its corresponding neglect of theory. A more recent criticism by Parsons challenges the whole basis of the Hawthorne studies, arguing that the 'Hawthorne effect' resulted from operant conditioning which was revealed in the way in which production results were constantly fed back to the operators (Parsons 1974).

Nevertheless, the impact of Mayo's work can scarcely be exaggerated and it is generally regarded as among the most important in the whole field of the social sciences. As Haire points out:

> 'It was no longer possible to see a decrement in productivity simply as changes in illumination, physical fatigue and the like. It was no longer possible to look for explanation of turnover simply in terms of an economic man maximising dollar income. The incentive to work was no longer seen as simple and unitary but rather infinitely varied, complex and changing.'
> (Haire 1954:376)

2 Sherif and the formation of group norms

By the middle of the 1930s a burst of activity took place in the United States concerning empirical research on groups. Moving away from simply accumulating data, researchers began to experiment in areas which, until then, were often treated as 'mystical' and outside the range of legitimate scientific study. In 1936, Sherif published a book containing a systematic theoretical analysis of the concept of 'social norms' which referred to the customs, traditions, standards, and other criteria of conduct (Sherif 1936). He related social norms to the psychology of perception, seeing the former as the frame of reference which a person brings to a situation and influencing the way in which he perceives it. In an experimental situation he employed the 'autokinetic effect' which describes the phenomenon which occurs in complete darkness, when a point of light appears to move even though it is, in fact, stationary.

In the first part of the experiment, individuals in a dark room observed a point of light and they had to estimate the distance of perceived movement. Nineteen subjects each made 100 judgements and it was discovered that 'the subjects subjectively established a range and a point within that range which is peculiar to the individual.' (Sherif 1972: 324). Further experiments showed that over a period of time, once a range was established, it tended to be preserved. Sherif concluded that in the absence of an external point of reference, each individual builds up an internal subjective reference point and each successive judgement is given in relation to that reference point. But what would happen if the experiment was carried out by people in a group? In the second part of the experiment this is precisely what happened. Groups of two and three people estimated the distance the light moved and then gave their answer verbally to Sherif. Surprisingly, in the group situation the individual results tended towards a common range. Each person was unwittingly influenced by the result given by the other group members and consequently their scores became closer and closer. In other words, a group norm was established. This is illustrated in *Figures 1a* and *1b* (see over), which clearly shows how estimates made by individuals on their own were significantly different, but then tended to become similar when the individuals were in a group.

Of equal importance, Sherif showed that if the experiment commenced in the group situation, then not only did the results tend to be similar, showing the 'group norm' effect, but this effect also continued even when the individual was no longer in the group situation. The group norm continued to influence behaviour even when the individual was not in the group. This is illustrated in *Figures 1c* and *1d* (see over).

Sherif's study is important for two reasons. First, it reveals and demonstrates the causes and influences of the group situation on individual behaviour. The norms of a group affect what the individual does in the group and this is a process of fundamental importance to the understanding of group behaviour. Second, this study shows that groups and group behaviour can be studied experimentally in a controlled situation and has helped to establish the view held among psychologists that group phenomena has a tangible reality that can be examined by the scientific method.

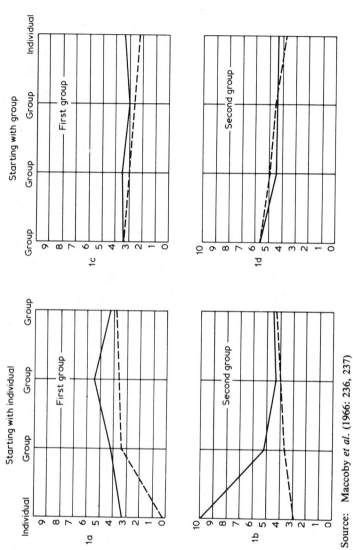

Figure 1 Medians in groups of two subjects

Source: Maccoby *et al.* (1966: 236, 237)

3 *Newcomb and the Bennington studies*

Between 1938 and 1939, Newcomb was also involved in investigating the same field of behaviour as Sherif, but in the 'real life' situation of Bennington College in America (Newcomb 1943). This college was opened in the 1930s and its formative period occurred during the intense social change associated with 'the New Deal'. Its women students were drawn largely from middle-class conservative families and they faced considerable changes in moving from a protected family life to the culture of the college. Newcomb, by using a variety of ingenious sociometric devices, was able to compare the influence of reference groups on students' attitudes as revealed in their attitude towards public affairs. His basic hypothesis was that 'in a membership group in which certain attitudes are approved individuals acquire the approved attitudes to the extent that the membership group (particularly as symbolized by leaders and dominant sub-groups) serves as a positive point of reference.' (Newcomb 1966: 262).

His investigation showed that the prevailing political atmosphere of the campus was 'liberal' and that the new students entering the college brought with them 'conservative' views which deviated from this. For instance in the 1936 Presidential election, 62 per cent of the freshmen 'voted' for the Republican candidate and 29 per cent for Roosevelt. Whereas, in the senior years, 14 per cent 'voted' Republican and 54 per cent 'voted' for Roosevelt. As might be anticipated, in this culture individual prestige was associated with non-conservatism and in an experiment to choose the student 'most worthy to represent the college', there was a direct correlation between the number of votes received and the 'liberal' views of the candidate.

Newcomb's study showed clearly that the attitudes of individuals are derived mainly from the groups to which they belong. The group puts strong pressure on its members to conform to its norms and evaluates them according to how they conform to them. Newcomb sums up the study in these words:

'In short, the Bennington findings seem to support the thesis that, in a community characterised by certain approved attitudes, the individual's attitude development is a function of the way in which he relates himself both to the total membership group and to one or more reference groups.'

(Newcomb 1966: 275)

4 *Lewin and the Democracy-Autocracy experiments*

Another significant piece of work was the experiment concerning children's behaviour under authoritarian and democratic leaders. This was carried out by Lippitt and White in 1939, under the enthusiastic guidance of Kurt Lewin, when all three were working at the Iowa Child Welfare Research Station (Lewin, Lippitt, and White 1939). Four boys' clubs, each with five members, met after school to engage in 'hobby' activities; these clubs were the subject of the experiment. Each club had a leader who was trained to work in one of three styles, 'autocratic', 'democratic', and 'laissez-faire' and the leaders rotated every six weeks. Observers made a full record of each club meeting and comparisons were made between the boys' behaviour under each leadership style. Many of the findings of this study were striking. For example, in the autocratic atmosphere, the boys were much more likely to lose initiative, to be restlessly discontented, to become aggressive and fight with each other, and to have no concern for group goals or the interests of other members. Preference for democratic leadership was clearly expressed by all but one of the twenty boys. The indirect effect of the autocratic style was also noticeable; the only four boys who dropped out did so during the autocratic period. It also induced more demand for attention, more destructive behaviour, and more scapegoating.

These experiments demonstrated a direct relationship between group atmosphere, determined by the leadership style, and tension levels in the individual group members. It also clearly showed how the social atmosphere affected the boys' sense of interdependence and interaction. Lewin found these studies highly significant and later wrote:

> 'There have been few experiences for me as impressive as seeing the expression on children's faces during the first day under an autocratic leader. The group that had formerly been friendly, open, co-operative and full of life, became within a short half-hour a rather apathetic-looking gathering without initiative. Autocracy is imposed on the individual. Democracy he has to learn!.'   (Marrow 1969: 127)

5 Conclusion — review of organization theory

This introduction has shown how the study of groups and organizations gradually grew into a significant and legitimate part of the total field of social psychology. Just as a biography of a famous person has to start with an analysis of the parents, so a study of group and organizational theory must begin with the apparently widely different pieces of work in which its origins can be found. These have been shown to include the work of philosophers, psychologists, psychoanalysts, sociologists, practical managers, and administrators. From those early beginnings, many writers and thinkers have continued to study groups and organizations from widely different aspects, and subsequently different schools of thought have developed.

A useful analysis of modern organization theories was made by Pugh who separated them into six categories (Pugh 1966):

(i) *Management theorists.* These include Fayol, Drucker, and Wilfred (now Lord) Brown, who have all attempted to describe their own managerial experience and from it develop general theories and prescriptions for more effective management and organization.

(ii) *Structural theorists.* In this area, there is the work of Weber, Selznick, Burns, and Stalker, who describe the relationship between organizational structure and such activities as task allocation, the exercise of authority, and the co-ordination of the various functions.

(iii) *Group theorists.* These include Mayo, Lewin, Lippitt, and Likert, who are all concerned with the influence of the immediate informal group on motivation and behaviour.

(iv) *Individual theorists.* Contributions in this area have been made by March, Simon, Herzberg, and Kelly, who have focused on: individual decision-making, motivation, and personal constructs, and also such concrete problems as selection, training, counselling, and job enrichment.

(v) *Technology theorists.* This area concentrates on the concept of the 'technology of manufacture', which is seen as a vital factor in the organization. Theorists in this area have been Taylor, Woodward, Trist, Miller, and Rice, the latter two use the concept of 'socio-technical' systems.

(vi) *Economic theorists.* Alfred Marshal in 1890 developed an economic theory of the firm, and since then, various people have looked at organizations from an economic and latterly a mathematical viewpoint, for example, Cyert, March, and Mains.

Group dynamics

With regard to theories about groups, an analysis has been made by Cartwright and Zander who list the different approaches to group dynamics in the following way (Cartwright and Zander 1960):

(i) Field theory

This approach stemmed specifically from the work and influence of Kurt Lewin. He used the concept of 'field' to describe all the interdependent forces that determine the behaviour of a person in what he called their 'life space'. Lewin was influenced by Gestalt psychology and used the mathematical branch of geometry called topology to describe the strength and direction of these forces. He has had a greater impact and influence on 'group dynamics' — a phrase he originated — than any other person, and his life and work will be described in Chapter 6.

(ii) Interaction theory

This approach sees a group as essentially a system of interacting individuals. The greatest influence in this area has been Robert Bales, who has developed a method for analysing individual's verbal contributions in terms of their categories, that is, asking for information, giving views, and so forth, which he then relates to behaviour and personality (Bates 1950).

(iii) Systems theory

General Systems Theory has influenced most disciplines and in Newcomb's work the central idea is 'systems of interlocking position and roles'. Workers in the Tavistock Institute, such as Rice, Trist, and Miller have used systems theory extensively to describe organizations in terms of an import, conversion, export process, and these will be explained in Chapter 8.

(iv) *Sociometric orientation*

This approach originated with Moreno and is concerned primarily with the interpersonal choices that bind groups of people together. By 1954, a large quantity of research had been carried out and was reviewed by Lindzey and Borgotta, who found that little systematic theory had evolved (Lindsey and Borgotta 1954).

(v) *Psychoanalytic theory*

This theory was first extended to group life by Freud and then by others, especially Scheidlinger and Bion. The main concepts dealt with are identification, anxiety, defence mechanisms, and the unconscious. This work mainly involves theories and concepts, rather than experimentation, and these ideas have permeated much of the work done in group dynamics.

(vi) *Cognitive theory*

Cognitive theory is, perhaps, the most influential of the major theories of human behaviour that have been developed in general psychology and then applied to groups. Strictly speaking it is not a theory but a 'point of view' that concentrates on the way in which information is received and integrated by the individual, and how this influences behaviour. A good example of this approach is the work of Festinger and his theory of 'cognitive dissonance' (Festinger 1957).

(vii) *Empiricist-statistical orientation*

This approach attempts to discover group concepts from such statistical procedures as factor analysis as opposed to *a priori* theories. Workers in this field make considerable use of techniques used in personality testing, and this approach is well illustrated by the work of Belbin, who has used it to construct effective management teams (Belbin, Aston, and Mottram 1976).

*

In spite of these different approaches and orientations, Cartwright and Zander believe that theorists and practitioners in the field of groups and group dynamics hold four basic assumptions in common (Cartwright and Zander 1960):

(i) Groups are inevitable and ubiquitous.
(ii) Groups mobilize powerful forces which produce effects of utmost importance to individuals.
(iii) Groups may produce both good and bad consequences.
(iv) A correct understanding of group dynamics — obtainable from research — permits the possibility that desirable consequences from groups can be deliberately enhanced.

The following chapters of this book will largely concentrate on a detailed examination of the fifth category of Cartwright's and Zander's classification, that is, 'psychoanalytic theory', and will attempt to survey the influence of psychoanalytic thought on the study of group and organizational behaviour. Other influences will be described which are not specifically psychoanalytic. For instance, the work and influence of Kurt Lewin must be described, because although he was a psychologist and not an analyst, his original and powerful influence underlies almost all studies of groups. General systems theory will also be examined, because of its profound influence on workers in the psychoanalytic field.

However, the main study will concentrate on such thinkers as Freud, Klein, and Bion and the way in which their original thinking has been developed by other workers into an influential body of thought and practice. These ideas continue to make a significant contribution to the study of the behaviour of people as they live and work together in all the different variety of groups and organizations in which most of us spend so much of our time.

2 The leader — the influence of Sigmund Freud

Group Psychology and the Analysis of the Ego

In 1921 Freud published his book *Group Psychology and the Analysis of the Ego*. In terms of Freud's thinking, it forms the middle of a trio of books, which contain some of his most seminal ideas. In the previous year, he had published *Beyond the Pleasure Principle* in which he first introduced his theory of the 'death instinct': the morbido as opposed to the libido. In 1923 he wrote *The Ego and the Id* in which he revised his account of the structure of the mind with the division into Id, Ego, and Super-Ego.

There are three reasons why *Group Psychology and the Analysis of the Ego* is important in the study of group behaviour:

(i) It offers a theory of group working, which is original and consistent within the whole framework of Freudian psychoanalytic theory.

(ii) It provides ideas that have become the starting point for later thinkers and from which major developments have been made.

(iii) It shows how psychoanalytic thought has always been concerned with social psychology (man in relationship) as well as individual psychology (man as a discrete personality).

Prior to the publication of *Group Psychology and the Analysis of the Ego*, various writers had published works attempting to provide theory and evidence about social man. In 1916 Trotter wrote *Instincts of the Herd in Peace and War* in which he put forward his theory of the 'herd instinct', stating that man has four primary instincts, — self-preservation, nutrition, sex, and the herd.

In 1920 two important books were published: Le Bon's *The Crowd: A Study of the Group Mind* and McDougall's *The Group Mind*.

In this setting, Freud's work on group psychology can be seen not only as a further extension of his own thoughts, but also as a response to other ideas which arose from different origins. In *Group Psychology and the Analysis of the Ego*, Freud analysed these ideas and evaluated them against psychoanalytic theory.

The basic question which Freud attempted to answer concerns the nature of the social instinct in man. Do human beings form groups and behave in a social manner because of a basic instinct that is 'given' by man's very nature and that is, therefore, not capable of further dissection? Or is the social instinct and group behaviour an expression of other, more primary, instincts?

Freud posed the problem as three distinct questions:

(a) What is a 'group'?
(b) How does it acquire the capacity for exercising such a decisive influence over the mental life of the individual?
(c) What is the nature of the mental change which it forces upon the individual?

Freud began with a close analysis of Le Bon's book *The Crowd*. Le Bon said that the difference between individual and group behaviour comes from 'a sort of collective mind' — the group constitutes a new 'provisional being' made up of each individual member and in this way individual cells combine to form a new organism. He also said that in the group the distinctive, conscious acquirements of each individual fall away, so that a sort of racial or collective unconscious emerges that forms the basis of the group's cohesion and action.

Other forces at work in the group, said Le Bon, are those of 'contagion' and 'suggestibility', the latter being akin to the hypnosis situation. He explored the concept of 'group mind' and said that it shows a similarity with the mental life of children and primitive people.

As a result of his careful analysis of Le Bon's work, which he regarded as 'deservedly famous', Freud posed two questions that were vital to the formulation of his final theory. First, if there is a collective mind, what is the bond that unites the group? Le Bon had provided nc answer to this. Second, if suggestibility is a factor in group behaviour, akin to the situation in hypnosis, who then is the 'hypnotist' in the group?

Freud then proceeded to review McDougall's book *The Group Mind*. McDougall argued that the factor of organization is the major influence on groups, and said that a crowd needs a common purpose in order to become a group. For McDougall, emotional contagion is the most important process in a group, leading to the intensification of a group's emotion, which he called 'the principle of direct induction of emotion by way of the primitive sympathetic response'. McDougall viewed an 'unorganized' group very unsympathetically, and referred to it as excessively emotional, impulsive, violent, fickle, inconsistent and irresolute and extreme in action' (McDougall 1920: 45). Having given five principal conditions for raising the collective mental life of such a group to a higher level, he said that all intellectual tasks should be withdrawn from the group and dealt with by individuals!

Freud's final and crucial criticism of McDougall and Le Bon was that their basic explanation revolved around the concept (Freud calls it 'the magic word') of 'suggestion', which they regarded as an irreducible phenomenon but which he found extremely unsatisfactory. 'There has been no explanation of the nature of suggestion, that is, of the conditions under which influence without adequate logical foundation takes place' (Freud 1922: 37).

At this stage, Freud made his original and seminal contribution to the debate by introducing the concept of libido in order to explain group behaviour. 'Libido is the energy of those instincts to do with all that may be comprised under the word "love"' (Freud 1922: 37), and he argued that the binding force of a group derives from the emotional ties of the members that are expressions of the libido. The two examples he used were the Church and the Army. Each of these groups has a head, Christ in the Church and the Commander-in-Chief in the Army, and each are believed to love the members of their own group equally. Each individual, therefore, has a libidinal tie with his leader and consequently a similar tie with every other member of the group.

One of the mechanisms involved in these libidinal processes is 'identification'; the process whereby a person wants to be like someone else, in the same way that a small boy wishes to grow up like his father. Freud claimed that: 'identification is known to psychoanalysis as the earliest expression of an emotional tie with another person' (Freud 1922: 60). In the process of identification, the person wishing to be like the other person, 'introjects' that person into the ego. This concept of 'introjection' was first put forward by Ferenczi, one of Freud's earliest collaborators. Ferenczi believed that the infant is inclined to make pleasant experiences part of his own self — introjection, while those which are painful are wished away — projection. Therefore in a group the common tie is based on an 'introjective identification' by every member with the leader. For instance, in the Church each Christian takes Christ into himself as his ideal and identifies himself with Him. Yet how does the ego deal with the introjected object that, in the group situation, is the leader? At this point Freud made use of his earlier concept — the 'ego ideal'. According to Freud, the ego differentiates itself into two parts, the ego and the ego ideal, the latter dealing with self-observation, the moral conscience, the censorship of dreams, and is the chief influence in repression. (In his book *The Ego and the Id*, Freud replaced the ego ideal with the concept of the super-ego.) In the process of identification, the object is introjected into the ego ideal, either adding to it or replacing it. For instance, in Freud's example of the Army, each soldier identifies with the Commander-in-Chief and replaces his ego ideal with the leader. Another example is that of two people in love. For Freud, when one is in love the ego can become either enriched — through introjection, or impoverished — the ego surrenders itself completely to the object and, in fact, replaces the ego ideal by the object.

Summing up these various ideas concerning the libido, the ego ideal, and the process of introjective identification, Freud combined them to say this: 'A primary group is a number of individuals who have substituted one and the same object for their ego ideal and have consequently identified themselves with one another in their ego' (Freud 1922: 80). He illustrated this statement with the following diagram:

Figure 2 The formation of a group

Source: Freud (1922: 80)

The group and the primal horde

So far, Freud had used the concept of the libido, in order to understand group behaviour, by looking at the earliest form of an emotional tie found in childhood, namely identification. By analogy, the relationship between a child and its father resembles the relationship between the leader and the members of the group or, at least, the same basic psychic processes are assumed to be operating in both situations. Freud then brought further insights to bear by looking at the original human tribe.

As stated earlier, in *Totem and Taboo* (1912) Freud had attempted to bring psychoanalytic theory to bear on anthropological material. He looked in particular at what he called the 'primal horde', where the group, ruled over by a despotic leader, eventually killed the leader and formed a community of brothers. A group can be said to resemble a revival of the primal horde: 'The leader of the group is still the primal father: the group still wishes to be governed by unrestricted force' (Freud 1951: 99). In *Totem and Taboo* Freud suggested that the primal horde actually *ate* the leader, thereby incorporating his 'strengths' into themselves. In the group the leader is incorporated into each individual, not by eating, but by the process of introjective identification. 'The primal father is the group ideal which governs the ego in the place of the ego ideal' (Freud 1922: 100). This, said Freud, also explains hypnosis. The hypnotist, when he commands the subject to sleep, puts himself in the place of the subject's parent and re-awakens the basic compliant relationship towards his father. In other words, the hypnotist becomes the subject's ego ideal.

Following this analysis of 'group psychology', the major points made by Freud may be summarized thus:

(i) The major force operating in a group is the libido: the sexual instinct operating within every individual which is basic to his behaviour and is not capable of further dissection. This does not mean or imply that group behaviour is sexual, in the usual meaning of the word. In the normal nature of things, the libido finds its most obvious expression in the sexual union of a man and woman. However, as Freud said, 'in other circumstances, they [the sexual instincts] are diverted from this aim or are prevented from reaching it, though always preserving enough of their original nature to keep their identity recognizable (as in the longing for proximity and self-sacrifice)' (Freud 1922: 38).

(ii) The group is bound together through libidinal ties to the leader and to the other members of the group.

(iii) The emotional bonds in the group derive essentially from 'identification', which Freud described as the earliest expression of an emotional tie with another person.

(iv) The process of identification involves the 'introjection' of the admired or loved object into the ego ideal. In the group, this object is the leader with whom each member identifies, and having the same object in their ego ideals, they can identify with each other.

(v) The leader of the group is like the leader of the primal horde and is able to exercise his authority in the group because he is now the group ideal, each member having replaced his own ego with him.

The book is clearly rich in new insights, new ideas, and hypotheses and places the study of group behaviour and group psychology firmly within the total framework of psychoanalytic thought. It opens up new pathways of thought, which were later to be developed and explored by Klein and other workers in this field. For instance, the concept of introjective identification and the development of the ego become of major importance in the development of theory about the Oedipus complex and the formation of the super-ego.

However, the book presents one concept that is not fully developed and appears to contain certain inconsistencies. This is the concept of identification — the process by which relationships are formed. The examples which Freud gave to illustrate groups bound together by identification were the Army and the Church.

The members of both groups identify with their leaders — the Commander-in-Chief and Christ respectively — introject these leaders into their egos who now become, by replacement, their ego ideals, and consequently they themselves identify with each other in their egos.

However, these examples, on closer examination, appear to illustrate different processes. In the Church, the leader, who is Christ, is incorporated into every member and becomes each member's ego ideal: this example illustrates the process of identification by introjection exactly. But does the example of the Army illustrate the same process?

Freud gave a further example when he talked of being in love and the process of idealization. He said, 'We see that the object is being treated in the same way as our own ego, so that when we are in love a considerable amount of narcissistic libido overflows on to the object' (Freud 1922: 74). Clearly, the process of identification in this case is not one of introjection but an outgoing process; in this instance Freud's diagram (see p. 19) needs the arrows reversed, that is, the movement is from the ego to the object and not vice versa. Freud, in fact, was aware of this apparent difference and offered a tantalizingly brief discussion in just two pages of the final chapter, headed 'Postscript'. He made the distinction between:

(a) identification of the ego with an object, and
(b) replacement of the ego ideal by an object.

Nevertheless, even this fails to solve the problem. For he argued that in the Army, while the soldiers take their superior as their ideal resulting in bonds of comradeship between them, they do not identify with their superior. 'But he [the soldier] becomes ridiculous if he tries to identify himself with the General.' Whereas in the Church, the members identify with Christ as well as loving each other.

The feeling remains that Freud provided one explanation for two distinct (though related) processes. Identification by introjection explains the bonding that is formed by members of the Church between each member and their leader, Christ, and consequently between each other. However, it fails to explain the bonding between a group such as the Army, or a couple 'in love', where the affective flow appears to be in the opposite direction, that is, from ego to object.

3 Transference and projection — the influence of Ferenczi

In the previous chapter it was shown that central to Freud's theory of group behaviour is the concept of 'identification by introjection': the psychological process whereby the members of a group, wishing to identify with the leader, incorporate his ideas and attitudes and make them their own. They 'introject' the leader into that part of themselves which Freud calls the ego-ideal — this is shown diagrammatically on p. 19.

However, this is essentially a one-way process and does not explain situations where the movement is apparently in the reverse direction, that is, from the group member towards the leader, such as between a soldier and his commander-in-chief. When Freud used the term 'introjection' he acknowledged that the idea originated from another psychologist, Ferenczi. It will be useful to analyse precisely what Ferenczi said on this subject in order to see if further information can be obtained.

Ferenczi was an analyst and hypnotist who was greatly influenced by Freud's ideas. Although he did not write specifically about groups he was concerned with the primary nature of relationships, trying to understand the basis of bondings between people. In 1916 he published a major book *Contributions to Psychoanalysis* that contains a chapter called 'Introjection and Transference'.

Ferenczi attempted to apply the ideas of psychoanalysis to everyday life in order to explain ordinary behaviour. For Ferenczi, the difference between neurotic and normal behaviour is one of degree and not of kind. He began by using Freud's idea of 'transference' which he calls 'one of his most significant discoveries'. Transference refers to the highly emotional relationship that invariably develops between the client and the analyst during· an analysis. Because the strength of these emotions (love, hate, dependency, resentment, and so forth) are frequently more powerful than the situation calls for, they reveal complex processes at work, which appear to be different from those of ordinary relationships. Freud had already drawn attention to this phenomena and saw it as a process central to the analysis. The patient was in fact 'transferring' on to the analyst fears, hates, and loves that until then were repressed in the unconscious, but were released in the analytic situation and transferred on to the analyst. A recognition of transference and an analysis of these transferred feelings leading to their resolution, rapidly became (and has remained) the central feature in Freudian psychoanalysis.

However, Ferenczi expanded this idea by saying that the process of transference does not only happen in analysis but in fact is part of everyday living. 'The daily occurrence of a simple civic life offers the neurotic the richest opportunity for the displacement on to permissible fields of impulses that are incapable of being conscious' (Ferenczi 1916: 32).

In other words, people are continually transferring their own repressed feelings on to other people and Ferenczi gave many illustrations taken from religious and political movements. He was then able to put forward a theory that combined the two psychological processes of transference and projection. He first considered the behaviour of paranoics and neurotics.

The paranoic, he wrote, gets rid of his unpleasant feelings and 'projects' them (that is, transfers them) on to the external world. The neurotic, on the other hand, does the exact opposite and takes in, that is, 'introjects', part of the outside world into his ego. However, Ferenczi considered pathological behaviour to be only an extreme form of the behaviour of normal people.

> 'We came to the conclusion that the paranoic projection and the neurotic introjection are merely extreme cases of psychical processes, the primary forms of which are to be demonstrated in every normal being.
>
> Besides projection, introjection is significant for man's view of the world.' (Ferenczi 1916: 41)

Using these twin processes of identification, Ferenczi applied them to the earliest behaviour of an infant, seeing them as the way in which the new-born infant gradually learns to distinguish a reality which is separate from his ego and not subject to his will. In fact he called these earliest processes 'the primordial projection'. He also used these ideas to explain the original formation of the concepts of good and bad in the infant. 'The first object-love and the first object-hate are, so to speak, the primordial transferences [projections], the root of every future introjection.' (Ferenczi 1916: 42).

Conclusion

It may seem that these rather complex ideas of Ferenczi have little, if anything, to do with understanding the behaviour of people in groups and organizations. However, the following chapters will show that the concepts of identification by projection and introjection did, in fact, become central and basic to the development of a theory of group behaviour. They also begin to reveal that group behaviour is individual behaviour writ large. Unlike sociology, psychoanalysis explains group and organizational behaviour in terms of *intra*-personal behaviour, that is, in terms of what is going on inside the psyche of each individual.

Specifically, Ferenczi showed that organizational life can be the expression of the individual's unconscious impulses through the processes of identification. He also used these ideas to explain the formation of the first 'object-relationships' in the infant, resulting in the identification of 'good' and 'bad'.

4 The child's world of the adult — the contribution of Melanie Klein

Psychoanalytic theory has always been concerned with the behaviour of the child as a key to understanding the behaviour of the adult. However, in order to understand a child's behaviour, it is necessary to understand the child's world and to realize that it is not simply the adult's world in miniature. For instance, the adult's world is filled with many people who are recognized through an intricate network of relationships. This world is filled with thousands of objects and people and these combine to form a myriad of experiences providing pain or pleasure, happiness or sadness, together with a host of less intense feelings that often pass unnoticed.

Freud helped people to understand that the child's world is simpler than the adult's, containing only a small number of objects and, more importantly, inhabited by only one or two people who dominate it. This world provides only intense experiences, with sharply defined feelings of pain or pleasure that can completely flood the child's emotions.

In the child's world, much of what happens, happens for the first time and each new beginning creates the nucleus around which patterns of behaviour start to form. Thus, the child's relationship with its mother (or the parental figure) is of crucial importance because it is the first relationship ever formed and in some way influences the formation of all future relationships.

Freud concentrated in particular on the three- and four-year-olds as he believed that at this stage the initial sexuality of the child begins to show in what he called the Oedipus complex.

Many people found (and still find) it difficult to accept theories based on the supposed psychological processes of a three-year-old.

However, new theories and concepts of behaviour were soon to be developed, based on the behaviour of babies rather than children. Melanie Klein, a psychoanalyst, initially followed Freud in describing her work and ideas in terms of his structural theory of the psychic apparatus: the ego, super-ego, and id. However, from her work with very young children she developed the technique of analysing their play in terms of their anxieties and phantasies and this led her to develop new ideas, some of which differed from Freud.

Klein's theories are complex and sophisticated and have aroused either intense opposition or complete devotion; the latter leading to a strong school of 'Kleinian' analysts. Ernest Jones, a co-worker with Freud and author of his official biography, described how Klein's views split the British Psycho-Analytic Society into two extreme groups. The opposition declared that her conclusions not only diverged from, but were also incompatible with, the conclusions of Freud. Should she be classed with the other 'heretics' such as Adler, Jung, Stekel, and Rank who, according to Jones, had separated from Freud, not because of more profound insights, but because they were 'influenced by subjective motives — a rationalisation of inner resistances'! (Jones 1948: 10). Nevertheless Jones gave Klein his *imprimatur*, agreeing in general with her ideas and said that in the field of psychoanalytic theorizing, Klein's work was likely to play a very central part. Certainly this has proved to be true.

Evidence for her theory

As stated earlier, Klein's ideas and theories resulted from her observation of young children and she developed a new play technique which enabled her to analyse their behaviour. She discovered, for instance, that in two- and three-year-olds there was strong evidence of the operation of the super-ego, frequently with very savage characteristics.

This evidence conflicted with Freud's theory concerning the Oedipus complex. He had argued that at about three to four years of age, the childish libidinal instincts became prominent as the boy seeks to displace his father in order to gain the love of his mother (vice versa for the girl). Involved in this process is the formation of the super-ego: the child introjects the parental figure which becomes internalized and from then on acts as the conscience and internal censor of the ego. Following the working through of the Oedipus complex, the child enters the latency period when the sexual instincts lie dormant, until they re-emerge in adolescence to develop into mature adult sexuality. The Oedipal stage is of vital importance to the individual, affecting as it does object-relations, the formation of the super-ego, and the development of full genital sexuality. Clearly, if the child's experiences during this time are contrary to the successful working through of the Oedipus situation, the effects will be shown in later life in neurosis and psychosis.

Freud had developed this theory based on material presented to him during analysis which invariably involved adults. However, Klein's observations indicated that these processes were already developed and operating in two- and three-year-olds; consequently she was forced to look for the development of the super-ego in the earliest days of life. Eventually, she decided that these important developments of behaviour occurred in the first six months of life.

The world of the child

Klein attempted to conceptualize and describe the mental processes that were taking place in the mind of the baby from the first days of its birth. Freud had argued that the child's world is relatively simple but Klein maintained that the infant's world is extremely basic, consisting of only one object, namely the mother's breast. The first relationship the infant has is not with the mother as a whole person, but with only a part of her, the breast. In Klein's theory, this is the primal relationship which influences the formation and development of all future relationships.

The breast is the only object in the infant's world and it can be the source of complete and utter satisfaction or, if withheld, complete frustration and anger. It is difficult for an adult to imagine a world in which there is only one object and where that object can provide such intense feelings. However, this is the world of the baby as perceived by Klein in her attempt to understand and describe the processes that occur in the infant's mind in the earliest days of life. Her hypothesis states that these earliest processes, which develop in this elemental situation, continue to operate in adult life and can be used as the basic explanation for both normal and abnormal behaviour.

Projective identification

Central to Klein's theories are the twin psychological mechanisms of projective and introjective identification and she used these to describe the processes by which the earliest object-relationships are formed. In Chapter 2 it was shown that Freud used the idea of introjection to describe how members of a group identify with the leader and consequently with each other. As stated in Chapter 3, Ferenczi, working from the concept of transference, made projection and introjection twin processes in the development of the normal person. However, Klein acknowledged Freud as the source of her ideas and did not mention Ferenczi in this context. She said, 'On re-reading *Group Psychology and the Analysis of the Ego*, it appears to me that he [Freud] was aware of identification by projection, although he did not differentiate it by means of a special term from identification by introjection' (Klein, Heimann, and Money-Kyrle 1955: 313, footnote).

Jaques, a 'Kleinian' analyst, went even further:

'In *Group Psychology and the Analysis of the Ego* he [Freud] establishes both processes of identification — that is to say identification by introjection of the object, and identification by projection into the object. Indeed it is in that book that the process later called "projective identification" by Melanie Klein is first described.'   (Jaques 1970: 217)

It appears that less than justice is done by both these writers to the thought and influence of Ferenczi, who was using these terms and concepts as early as 1909.

The paranoid-schizoid position

Klein's description of the origins of behaviour involves three basic concepts. The first is the ego, the central part of the self which is the 'manager' of the psyche, mediating between what is inside the self and what is in the external world. According to Klein, the ego is in existence from the start of life even though, at that stage, it is rudimentary, fragile, and liable to fluctuate between an integrated and fragmented state. The second concept is the libido, the life force which includes all those feelings usually associated with the word 'love'. The third concept is the controversial one of the death instinct, the morbido as opposed to the libido. This idea had appeared in Freud's later writings and although it was (and still is) a bone of contention among analysts, Klein was convinced of its existence.

At the start of life the infant experiences anxiety through the operation of the death instinct, which is felt as a fear of annihilation and persecution. It is here that Klein used the twin concepts of projection and introjection to explain the next stages. The infant identifies these feelings of persecutory anxiety with the only object present in its world, namely the mother's breast, and projects these unpleasant feelings into it. Thus the breast is experienced as persecutory, an external uncontrollable object. This is then introjected into the rudimentary ego, where it becomes an internal persecutor, 'reinforcing the fear of the destructive impulse within' (Klein 1946: 100).

However, in reality the breast provides the infant with intense feelings of bliss and satisfaction during feeding. Klein supposed then that the infant experiences the breast as providing two completely different kinds of feelings and consequently relates this to two completely different objects: 'the good breast' and 'the bad breast'. This is achieved by the process of 'splitting' which is a concept central to Klein's theories. The ego 'splits' the object, getting rid of the 'bad' breast by projecting it outwards and keeping the 'good' breast by introjecting it into the ego. In splitting the breast, the infant phantasizes a good, satisfying breast and introjects this good breast completely. This then becomes, for the infant, the first internal good object and acts as a focal point in the ego. At the same time, the breast is perceived as 'bad' — frustrating and persecutory — both as an external threatening object and as an internalized threat within the ego.

Here then is the formation of the earliest object-relations and the earliest experiences of love and hate and of good and bad. Klein's theory gives a rather bewildering picture of the dynamic phantasy of the infant's earliest mental processes, involving external and internal objects, but even so the reality of the infant's situation profoundly affects these processes. For, the degree of satisfaction the breast actually provides determines the extent to which the internalized 'good breast' is strengthened in the ego, and the infant's libido can be projected into the external breast. When this does not happen, the infant's anxieties concerning the fear of the external 'bad breast' are increased, resulting in sadistic attacks (in phantasy) on the breast and increased persecutory fears of the internalized bad breast.

These processes, involving splitting, projection, and introjection, are taking place in the infant's phantasy. Nevertheless, the results are real in that the split-off object is in relationship with the ego and hence splitting the object involves splitting the ego. As Klein stated: 'I believe that the ego is incapable of splitting the object — internal and external — without correspondingly a splitting within the ego taking place' (Klein 1946: 101). The end result is that feelings and relations are cut off from one another.

In a way, it is as if the primal fight between life and death takes place in the mental life of every infant. Death, in the form of the death instinct, is deflected away from the ego by means of splitting and projection. Life, in the form of the libido, can be seen as the way in which the good object is internalized and results in loving feelings projected outwards. According to Klein: 'As regards splitting the object, we have to remember that in states of gratification love feelings turn toward the gratifying breast, while in states of frustration, hatred and persecutory anxiety attach themselves to the frustrating breast' (Klein 1946: 101). However, splitting involves work, the expenditure of psychic energy necessary to keep the good and bad objects apart. It is only as the real breast provides satisfaction that the internalized good object can begin to counteract splitting and this results in a drive towards cohesiveness and integration in the ego.

Alongside this process of splitting, which Klein called the earliest defence mechanism against anxiety, are the related processes of 'idealization' and 'denial'. The more the persecutory anxiety is experienced, the more the good aspects of the breast are exaggerated, resulting in an idealized breast, capable of inexhaustible gratification. With this goes the complementary process of denying the bad breast and the painful feelings experienced in frustration. However, it is not only the denial of the bad object —

the object is in relation with the ego and, therefore, the process involves the denial and annihilation of part of the ego.

Klein called the first six months of life the 'paranoid-schizoid position'. It is paranoid because one of the major feelings experienced by the infant is persecutory anxiety and fear. It is schizoid because of the splitting of the ego and its fluctuations between an integrated and fragmented state. Klein saw these processes as psychotic and believed that, if the infant cannot work through this position, they re-emerge in later life as paranoia and schizophrenia. 'In schizoid personalities, the violent splitting of the self and excessive projection have the effect that the person towards whom this process is directed is felt as a persecutor' (Klein 1946: 104).

Yet, contained within these hypotheses is the idea that these infant psychotic processes are also the processes of normal development: 'The processes of splitting off parts of the self and projecting them into objects are thus of vital importance for normal development as well as for abnormal object relations' (Klein 1946: 103). Linked with this are projection and introjection, the optimal balance between these two processes vitally affect ego development.

To sum up what happens in the paranoid-schizoid position, a quotation from Segal gives the central points:

> 'As the processes of splitting, projection and introjection help to sort out his perceptions and emotions and divide the good from the bad, the infant feels himself to be confronted with an ideal object, which he loves and tries to acquire, keep and identify with, and a bad object, into which he has projected his aggressive impulses and which is felt to be a threat to himself and his ideal object.' (Segal 1973: 67)*

The depressive position

While Klein said that there is no clear division between the two stages of development, she postulated that the second stage of infant development commences in about the second half of the first year. Common parental experience reveals an observable

*Segal (1973) gives a complete bibliography of Klein's publications.

change in the infant's behaviour at this time, namely that he begins to recognize his mother, seeing her as a whole person. It is the concept of wholeness and the integration of parts, both in external objects and within the self, that are the essential characteristics of this stage. These processes are helped by the maturation of the central nervous system and general physiological development and growth.

The recognition of the mother as a whole object implies two aspects of psychic development. First, the child begins to relate to the mother as a whole object and not to part-objects, such as the breast, face, and so forth. Second, he begins to recognize that the good and bad experiences do not emanate from two separate sources, a good mother and a bad mother, but from one person who is the source of both.

As this recognition of the mother as a whole object develops, so the ego develops as an integrated whole, with a diminution of splitting and projection, leading to an 'increased understanding of psychic reality and better perception of the external world, as well as a greater synthesis between inner and external situations' (Klein 1946: 105).

As the infant begins to realize that the source of both his frustration and gratification are the same, he also realizes that he himself can love and hate this same person — his mother. The characteristic feelings in this position are depression, despair, and guilt due to the infant believing that he has damaged or may damage, has destroyed or may destroy, his loved object. Consequently, Klein calls this second stage 'the depressive position'.

As the infant works through this position, with the increasing integration of the ego and the establishment of a whole object relationship, there arises the drive for reparation, the wish to restore and repair what was felt to be destroyed by his own sadistic impulses. Just as the infant believed he had destroyed, so he now believes he can restore and make well and this results in a constant struggle between destructiveness and loving reparative impulses. If the loving impulses are successful and the mother's love strengthens, confirms, and returns these impulses, then the infant will experience renewed hope. This will lead to a further diminution of projection and splitting and the firm establishment of a super-ego, experienced as a source of love rather than as a severely persecuting object.

Implications for adult behaviour

Klein's detailed theories of the earliest mental processes in the life of the infant enabled her to use them to explain adult behaviour, both normal and abnormal. She had shown that the formation of the earliest relationship involved projective and introjective identification, linked with splitting and denial. Klein believed that normal adults, when experiencing situations of persecutory anxiety, revert to this earliest pattern of behaviour and use the processes of projective and introjective identification as a defence against their anxiety. An illustration of this could be the attack a man might make, either verbally or physically, against another male showing signs of homosexuality. Kleinian theory would explain this by saying that the attacker identifies those unresolved homosexual parts of himself with the overt homosexual, and projects them on to the latter. They are now externalized and expelled from him and, therefore, all the fear and hatred which was inside himself and self-directed can safely be vented on to the homosexual. In fact, the homosexual is merely the receptacle for the attacker's internal bad feelings.

Another example could be the way a teenager worships a 'pop' star. Since he wishes to be like the star, he identifies with him and introjects him, splitting off the bad parts and completely denying them, and idealizing the good aspects. Consequently, the teenager will have a viewpoint that completely denies any criticism of the person he idolizes. This process is not of course restricted to the young and the same processes can be used to explain the blind faith that is sometimes placed in political leaders.

Klein's theories can also be used to explain the behaviour of psychotics, especially paranoics and schizophrenics. The paranoic is someone who continually feels that people are persecuting him. He feels that the neighbours are talking about him or that some- one is trying to poison him. This can be explained by saying that, for some reason, the person as an infant was unable to work through the first 'paranoid-schizoid' position. As a result the adult continues to violently split the self and through excessive projection feels that the person towards whom this process is directed is persecuting him. In fact the persecutors are the bad objects in his own mind. The schizophrenic is the person who is unable to resolve the different parts of himself and still experiences a fragmented ego, frequently showing signs of depression because he is unable to resolve the opposing parts of the self and therefore can not work through the depressive position.

*

Clearly, the implications of Klein's theory are much wider than this chapter can cover. Yet it is important to realize the centrality that is given to the twin processes of projective and introjective identification. The next chapter will show how they form the core of a unique theory of group and organizational behaviour.

5 Groups and their basic assumptions — the influence of Wilfred Bion

Perhaps the most original theory of group and organizational behaviour was developed by Wilfred Bion who, together with Freud and Lewin, has provided a major source of theoretical influence. The main part of Bion's work was carried out when he was a member of the Tavistock Institute of Human Relations in London, and in a book describing the history of that Institute, Dicks wrote: 'most of us in the Tavistock circle would assign pride of place to Wilfred Bion's massive conceptual contribution to the theory and practice of group relations' (Dicks 1970: 309).

Bion, a practising psychoanalyst of the Kleinian school, still contributes to psychoanalysis by publishing a variety of books on the subject. However, his seminal work is a collection of papers published between 1943 and 1952 in which he related his various experiences with groups and gradually developed a complete theory.*

The Northfield experiment

In the last war Bion served as a psychiatrist with the Army and was put in charge of the training wing of Northfield hospital, a military psychiatric hospital involving about 100 men. He found that the soldiers' neuroses were revealed not only in low morale, dirty wards, and apathy, but also in the way in which he was

*These papers are now collected and published in one book — Bion (1968).

continually besieged by both patients and staff with apparent administrative problems that for Sofer were 'neurotic problems of persons writ large in organisational terms' (Sofer 1973: 703).

In approaching this problem, Bion reasoned that, in strict army terms (he had been a tank commander in the First World War, gaining the DSO), discipline could be restored if the men could unite against a common enemy. He perceived this common enemy to be 'the existence of neurosis as a disability of the community' and concluded that this neurosis should be displayed as a problem of the organization (a problem that was hindering the training wing from working effectively) and that members should be encouraged to work collectively in order to overcome it. The result was a six-week experiment, now known as the 'Northfield experiment', that was to provide the basis for Bion's future work with groups. A framework of discipline was laid down for the soldiers, which said that every man must join a group, such as map-reading, handicrafts, and so forth. There was also a compulsory daily parade, which developed into a kind of therapeutic seminar where the activities of the wing could be discussed objectively.

As the training wing became more self-critical, the patients took more initiative and responsibility. Morale began to improve, more groups developed, and the increased cleanliness of the wards was noticeable, so that Bion could say: 'despite the changing population, the wing had an unmistakeable esprit de corps' (Bion 1968: 21). The essential changes were that the men became increasingly concerned with their ability to make contact with reality, to form relationships with each other, and to work co-operatively and efficiently on a common task.

Implications of the experiment

The description of this brief experiment, first published in 1943, contained the seeds that were later to blossom into a comprehensive theory of group working (Bion and Rickman 1963). These are:

> (i) Individual psychology is fundamentally group psychology. Behaviour by one member of the group influences, and is influenced by, all the other members.

(ii) The rational working of the group is profoundly affected by the emotions and irrational feelings of its members. The full potential of the group is only released when this fact is recognized and dealt with.

(iii) Administrative and managerial problems are simultaneously personal and interpersonal problems expressed in organizational terms.

(iv) The group develops when it learns by experience in gaining greater contact with reality.

The emergence of a theory of group behaviour

In 1948 Bion started 'taking' groups at the Tavistock Clinic and his book *Experiences in Groups* (1968) describes these experiences and how he interpreted them. His initial reports showed that there was a great deal of boredom, apathy, and desultory conversation in the groups. The group members — some patients and some not — seemed to have one thing in common, namely, they were not getting what they expected and Bion was not behaving in the way they had hoped.

At this stage, it is important to see and understand Bion's behaviour in the group. In essence, he played the classic role of psychoanalyst giving interpretations of behaviour in order to make what was unconscious conscious, and bringing phantasy into the light of reality. However, the unique and innovative difference was that he treated the whole group as the patient, giving interpretations to the group and not to individuals. He said, very specifically, that group psychotherapy is not individual therapy done in public, but is directed to the group as a whole. He was clearly the leader of the group by virtue of being in the position of psychiatrist but, as he said: 'I take advantage of this position to establish no rules of procedure and to put forward no agenda' (Bion 1968: 77).

Bion's behaviour caused some confusion and bewilderment in the group and led him initially to isolate two aspects of group behaviour for consideration. The first was the futile conversation of the group which, he said, was almost devoid of intellectual content and critical judgement. This was due to the influence of powerful emotions in the group which nullified any effective work. The second concerned the nature of his own contributions: 'They would seem to be concerned with matters of no importance to anyone but myself' (Bion 1968: 40).

As Bion persisted with his method and gained more experience of group behaviour, he gradually perceived regularity and patterns in what initially had seemed random activity. His book shows the slow unfolding of his theories and their gradual evolution.

The theory of basic assumptions

Bion described various group meetings in which two people became involved in a conversation and to which the rest of the group appeared to give attentive silence. He suggested that the pair and the group held the basic assumption that the relationship was in some way a sexual one. This assumption was unspoken and may have been quite unrealistic. Nevertheless, it seemed that the pair and the group behaved 'as if' this assumption was true, held, and agreed by everyone. It became the unspoken and unconscious basis for their behaviour, both influencing and directing it, and to which all the group members subscribed. From this, Bion developed one of the central parts of his theory. Whenever the group is working, it can behave as if a basic assumption is held in common by all the members, and this will directly influence the activity of the group. Bion called this the 'basic assumption group'. By this he meant that the group was behaving in a particular mode, 'as if' all the members held a basic assumption in common. He believed that the basic assumption could colour, influence, and suffuse any rational work which the group attempted to do.

According to Bion, there are three distinct emotional states of groups from which three basic assumptions can be deduced. Only one basic assumption will be evidenced at any one time, although it can change three or four times in an hour or persist for three months. The first of these is the basic assumption of dependency (baD).

Dependency (baD)

When a group is working on the basic assumption of dependency it behaves as if 'the group is met in order to be sustained by a leader on whom it depends for nourishment, material and spiritual, and protection' (Bion 1968: 147). Consequently, the members of such a group behave as if they are inadequate and immature, knowing nothing and having nothing to contribute. At the same time, they act as if the leader is omnipotent and omniscient, someone who can solve all difficulties and problems as if by magic. Bion quoted a member from a group, which he was taking, that exactly illustrates this. On being asked why he did not contribute, the member replied: 'I do not need to talk because I know that I only have to come here long enough and all my questions will be answered without my having to do anything' (Bion 1968: 148). This basic assumption group is, therefore, hostile to any scientific method, for it acts as if power flows from the magic of the leader who may be idealized into some sort of god.

This cult of the all-powerful leader flourishes provided that someone is willing to play the role in the way the group desires. The group can also deify some idea or object, such as a 'bible' of the group's past events which then dominates its present activities. When these things occur, no learning nor any work can be achieved. For the basic assumption of dependency, in full operation, successfully defends the group from reality. The sole dynamic of the group's behaviour arises from the internal phantasies of the group, a sort of corporate madness in which every member colludes and which stifles any independent thought or co-operative work.

However, what happens in such a group when the leader fails to live up to the group's expectations? This must inevitably happen since no member of the group can possibly act as leader in the way the group's assumption demands. Anyone brave or foolish enough to attempt this role must, sooner or later, arouse the group's disappointment and hostility. This explains some of Bion's early experiences where the group clearly accepted him as the 'Doctor' who could cure all, but nevertheless ignored or rejected his contributions. The group was then in the basic assumption of dependency and Bion's behaviour did not fit the role of dependent group leader. Consequently, his words and his role were rejected with some hostility — he was refusing to collude in their unconscious phantasies.

According to Bion, when the group rejects a leader, because he fails them in their expectations, they appoint another one who is the sickest member: 'a thorough-going psychiatric case'. However, the same process will happen again, and the group will demote that leader and attempt to reinstate the former. This oscillation between believing that the leader is at one time 'good' and at another time 'bad', or 'mad' and then a 'genius', results in a highly emotional and explosive situation that may not be able to be contained within the group. It can spread to other groups and only ceases when enough outside groups have been drawn in to absorb the reaction. In practice, this may result in complaints being made to 'a higher authority', such as a letter written to a member of parliament.

There is another way in which a group in 'baD' can react to development demands, and that is to split into two sub-groups, thereby forming a schism. One sub-group, by manipulating the leader, whether a person, a 'bible', or a tradition, will ensure that support for the group demands no painful sacrifices and it may therefore become popular, although stagnant and dogmatic.

The other sub-group may behave differently, manipulating the leader so that membership becomes so demanding that no-one will wish to join. The objectives of both groups, however, are the same: to prevent reality intruding into their phantasies.

Pairing (baP)

When a group is working on the basic assumption of pairing, it behaves 'as if' the members have met together in order that two people can pair off and create a new, and as yet unborn, leader. This 'hoped-for' act of creation is essentially sexual, although the sex of the pair is unimportant. The pairing assumption group is characterized by hope, the hope that a Messiah will be born to deliver them from their anxieties and fears. This hope can be expressed in a variety of ways, such as that the coming season (it does not matter which) will be more agreeable than the present one, or the method of group therapy will revolutionize society, and so forth. Yet, within this very hope lies the seeds of future disappointment, for the hope exists only as long as the leader, whether Messiah or idea, remains unborn. 'Only by remaining a hope does hope exist' (Bion 1968: 152). In so far as the group succeeds in creating the leader, hope is weakened. For immediately this 'hoped-for' person or ideal will inevitably fail to deliver the group from their own fears, because these arise from within the group and include such emotions as destructiveness, hatred, and despair. Again, this basic assumption is essentially a defence mechanism of the group. It prevents the group from coming into contact with reality by keeping it a closed system. The dynamics arise entirely from within the group, allowing phantasies of what may happen to obscure what is actually happening. This allows the group to deny any difficult and possibly painful actions which a realization of what is actually happening must bring.

Fight/flight (baF)

The third basic assumption which can influence the group's behaviour is fight or flight, that is: 'the group has met to fight something or to run away from it. It is prepared to do either indifferently' (Bion 1968: 152). Bion said that fight or flight seem to be the only two techniques of self-preservation known by the group.

If a group is pre-occupied with this basic assumption, it will ignore all other activities or, failing this, it will attempt to suppress or run away from them. A leader is more important in this group than in the other two basic assumption groups, for action is essential to preserve the group. The person who accepts the role of leader in a fight/flight group must be prepared to lead the group against the common enemy and, where this does not exist, to create one. He is expected to recognize danger and enemies, and spur on his followers to courage and self-sacrifice. However, this leadership is based on paranoia: 'they' are endangering the group and 'they', wholly evil, have to be attacked and destroyed. Once the danger is passed, the leader is ignored and any statement made by him that does not involve fight or flight is also ignored. In Bion's concept, such a leader is entirely the creature of the group: 'the leader has no greater freedom to be himself than any other member of the group' (Bion 1968: 177). Again, the group operating on this assumption cannot develop or do useful work, because all its energies are concentrated on the group's phantasies. Reality is not tested, or rather it is deliberately kept at bay, for otherwise the group would have to deal with the frightening realization that the enemy that threatens them is not outside the group, but within.

The work group

In Bion's terms, the 'work group' refers to that aspect of group functioning that is the 'real' task of the group. Any group, whether the small group of a committee or a large group, such as the Army, has a specific, overt task to perform. To achieve this, the members of the group have to co-operate and use a sophisticated approach, organizing administrative and formal structures in order to achieve the task. Within this work group, certain ideas play a prominent part, such as development and the scientific method — however embryonic. In the basic assumption groups there is the underlying belief that an individual is fully equipped by instinct to play a full part in the group's activity. In the work group, however, members are aware that they have to learn and develop their skills, both personal and interpersonal, before they can make a full contribution. As a corollary, they realize that development results from taking part in such a group. This, perhaps, is the largest single difference between the two aspects of group functioning. The work group results in growth and development, the basic assumption group in stagnation and regression. The work group is in touch with reality, and in that mode the group operates as an open system, realizing that work has to be done to maintain the balance of forces between what is within the group and what is outside it. The basic assumption group acts as if it was a closed system, ignoring external reality and defending itself from it.

In this respect, Bion suggested that the characteristics of the work group are similar to the Freudian concept of the ego, which, as stated earlier, is that part of the mental apparatus that mediates between external reality and the rest of the self.

Another major difference between behaviour in the basic assumption group and the work group is revealed in the way in which people relate to one another. In the basic assumption group, Bion called this 'valency', 'the individual's readiness to enter into combination with the group in making and acting on the basic assumptions' (Bion 1968: 116). It is spontaneous and instinctive, requiring no effort and appears to be an inherent part of human behaviour. On the other hand, in the work group, a conscious effort has to be made by each individual to understand the other person as they work together. This is something very different from valency, implying a developing skill in human relations; Bion called this 'co-operation'. By combining the concept of the work group and the basic assumption groups, Bion was able to put forward a unique and comprehensive theory of group behaviour. This demonstrates that a group is able to function as a work group in which the members co-operate to achieve a common task and, because they are in touch with reality, develop and change as they succeed. Yet it also shows that the same group can operate as a basic assumption group, behaving as if the group had come together for pairing, for dependency, or for fight or flight. In this mode, the group uses its energy to defend itself from its own internal fears and anxieties, and consequently neither develops nor achieves any effective output.

It is important to realize that the work group and the basic assumption groups are not different groups containing different individuals, but the same individuals working in different modes. The emotions associated with each of the three basic assumptions can at any time suffuse the more rational working of the group. Conflict arises at the junction between the basic group and the work group.

Specialized work groups

Following these ideas, Bion put forward the idea of 'specialized work groups'. In effect these are sub-groups 'budded off' from the main group, whose main task is to deal with the basic assumptions on behalf of the main group, thereby allowing the work group function of the main group to proceed effectively. If society at large is taken as the main group, then various parts of it can be seen to be operating as specialized work groups. The Army can be seen as a specialized work group concerned with fight/flight. The Church is primarily concerned with dependency, and the aristocracy with pairing, that is, hoping for the birth of a genetically pure leader, presumably the monarchy. However, they are continually in danger of actually doing something, working as a work group rather than as a basic assumption group. To counteract this they have to disavow any achievement continually and must translate action into basic assumption mentality. Thus, the Church will say, *Non Nobis, Domine* (not unto us O Lord but unto thee be the glory) after a successful piece of work; the Army will encourage the belief that anything can be done by force, providing it is never used; and the aristocracy will insist that they (and the monarchy) are essentially democratic!

A psychoanalytic view of the group

Bion initially attempted to develop his theories in general terms rather than relating them specifically to psychoanalysis. As he wrote: 'I attempted deliberately, in so far as it is possible to a psycho-analyst admittedly proposing to investigate the group through psycho-analytically developed intuitions, to divest myself of any earlier psycho-analytic theories of the group in order to achieve an unprejudiced view' (Bion 1968: 165). He was not entirely successful in that aim. Underlying his concept of the work group and the basic assumption groups is basic Freudian theory. The group, when it is working rationally and co-operatively, is like the ego, mediating between reality and the self.

Like the ego, the work group can be influenced and, at times, overwhelmed by emotions arising from unconscious processes. In the group Bion played the role of analyst to the group as a whole, helping the group to bring these unconscious phantasies (unrecognized in the basic assumption group) into the arena of the work group, where they can be recognized and consciously dealt with in the 'here and now' in the way transference is dealt with in an individual analysis.

Yet how complete is Bion's theory so far? Are the basic assumption groups the final explanation which fully explain group processes and behaviours? Are they basic behavioural phenomena — cause and not effect?

Bion had already provided some clues that suggested that the basic assumption groups were interrelated in some way and could be the result of other, more primary, factors. He said: 'Sometimes it is convenient to think that the basic assumption has been activated by consciously expressed thoughts, at others in strongly stirred emotions, the outcome of proto-mental activity' (Bion 1968: 101).

For Bion, this 'proto-mental system' is a matrix of undifferentiated physical and psychological events, from which flow the emotions that are proper to any of the three basic assumptions. At the level of the proto-mental system, the group develops until its emotions become expressible in psychological terms, and it is only when specific events emerge as observable psychological phenomena that each of the basic assumptions can be differentiated. For Bion, their interrelation is such that not only does group phenomena reveal the operation of a specific assumption, it also implies a conspiracy between the work group and the operating basic assumption to confine the other two assumptions within the proto-mental system and not allow them to operate.

As well as this idea, the basic assumptions appear to have other common aspects, for example, they all include the existence of a leader. In the fight/flight assumption this is obvious. In the pairing assumption the leader, whether person or idea, remains unborn. In the dependency assumption a leader is required to play the role of magical god who can deliver the group from all ills. Yet, perhaps most importantly, the same emotions (such as fear, hate, suspicion, and anxiety) are apparent when any of the basic assumptions are operating. It is the combination of these emotions, including not only those revealed but also those suppressed, which are peculiar to each assumption. This evidence prepares the way for Bion to finalize his theory by putting forward his hypothesis regarding the behavioural mechanisms that underlie the basic assumptions.

Bion and Melanie Klein

It will be remembered that central to Klein's theories is the concept of projective identification, and the way in which adult behaviour can regress to infantile mechanisms characteristic of the paranoid-schizoid and depressive positions. Bion used these concepts to complete and underpin his theory of groups, seeing them not only as individual but also as group phenomena. It is essential to realize that he placed these mechanisms and processes at the very centre of group behaviour: 'Without the aid of these two sets of theories I doubt the possibility of any advance in the study of group phenomena' (Bion 1968: 8).

Bion believed that the source of the main emotional drives in the group arose through the processes described by Klein. The persecutory anxiety and fear, characteristic of the infantile position, occurs in the group when the members of that group are faced by the reality of their own behaviour. To protect themselves from these fears and 'in his contact with the complexities of life in a group the adult resorts, in what may be a massive regression, to mechanisms described by Melanie Klein as typical of the earliest phases of mental life' (Bion 1968: 141).

The group also provides another stimulus to these processes in that, according to Bion, it can approximate very closely to the mother's body in the mind of the individual. This provides the situation for mechanisms characteristic of the paranoid-schizoid position to operate, so that splitting of both the ego and the object will occur, together with projective identification and denial.

These ideas help to explain the common properties of the basic assumptions and reveal that they are not in fact basic, irreducible behavioural phenomena. They are specific expressions of psychotic anxiety within the group and are defence mechanisms against this anxiety. Their common basis is concerned with the mechanisms of splitting and projective identification, and the primitive anxieties of part-object relationships. These processes can help to explain how the leader of the group is created; this is not fully described in Freud's concept of identification by introjection. The process operating is the Kleinian concept of projective identification — each member splits off parts of his ego and projects them into the chosen leader. Thus, the leader and the group collude in their phantasies, with the leader, in fact, as much a creature of the group as the latter appears to be the puppet of the leader. This leader is chosen 'not by virtue of his fanatical adherence to an idea, but is rather an individual whose personality renders him peculiarly susceptible to the obliteration of individuality by the basic assumption group's leadership requirements' (Bion 1968: 177).

In the group dominated by the basic assumption of dependence, the mechanism at work is splitting, denial, and idealization. Good parts of the individuals are projected into the chosen leader and the bad parts denied. Hence, the leader can be idealized into a superhuman or god-like figure, with no bad or evil attributes, whose power is absolute and who works as if by magic.

The group, when it regresses and resorts to these Kleinian processes, is weakened in its ability to achieve a developmental contact with reality, in the way the primitive infantile ego is weakened and disintegrated when it resorts to splitting and projection in the paranoid-schizoid position. The more it attempts to separate 'the good group' from 'the bad group', idealizing the good and attacking, and fearing attack, from the bad, the more the individuals are resorting to their earliest relationship with part-objects. Like the infant working through the depressive position, the group, if it is to strengthen and develop, must realize that the good and the bad group is one and the same, and that ultimately the goodness and the badness is located within each individual. When that happens, the basic assumptions become inoperative and the work group triumphs.

The ancient myth of King Oedipus has always had a fascination for psychoanalysts because of the psychological truths it contains, and it still has power to illuminate group behaviour. In the story, Oedipus set out to discover and punish whoever was responsible for the dreadful crimes of matricide and incest. The final revelation came when he realized that these evil acts were carried out by himself and not by other people. In many ways this is a parable of projection, where the bad parts of the self are projected on to others who can then be persecuted and punished. The realization that these feelings originate within the self and represent internal persecutors can be terrifying, as terrifying as when Oedipus in his journeying met the Sphinx. The Sphinx was a monster who guarded 'the way' and asked a riddle of all travellers. Those who failed to answer were thrown over the cliff. The Sphinx asked Oedipus 'What walks with four legs in the morning, two legs in the afternoon and three legs in the evening?' Oedipus gave the correct answer: 'man himself', but this same sort of scientific questioning can still cause a group to experience the fear and terror which the dreadful Sphinx originally caused. An American analyst, Rioch, puts it this way: 'If the Sphinx were to ask "What is it that on Monday is wrangling, cruel and greedy; on Tuesday is indifferent and lazy; on Wednesday is effectively and intelligently collaborative?" one could easily answer, "That is man and it is also man in the group".' (Rioch 1970: 66).

Bion's theories are essentially optimistic in the sense that all psychoanalytic method involves a belief in development, change, and improvement. For once the group faces reality, it realizes that it is facing itself and this causes its terrors and anxieties to flee, just as Oedipus by answering 'man' put the Sphinx to flight. Bion wrote: 'I think one of the striking things about a group is that despite the influence of the basic assumptions, it is the work group that triumphs in the long run' (Bion 1968: 77). If these ideas seem somewhat obscure and theoretical, then the balance can be redressed by a quotation by Rice, spoken when he addressed a highly practical and work orientated conference.

'Work groups can behave with sophistication and maturity, and we can use the basic assumptions to assist task performance; the emotions associated with one basic assumption are then used to control and suppress the emotions associated with others. Mature work groups expect their leaders to mobilize the appropriate assumption for task performance. If the appropriate assumption is dependent, the leader has to be dependable but realistic; if pairing, potent, but with due regard to the limitations of his potency; if fight, constructively aggressive, brave but not foolhardy; if flight, able to extricate the group from a difficult situation, but no coward; nor must he expect to be able to solve all the group's problems in the process of extrication.'   (Rice 1965: 27)

Bion's theory of group processes is shown in diagrammatic form in *Figure 3*.

Figure 3 Bion's theory of group behaviour

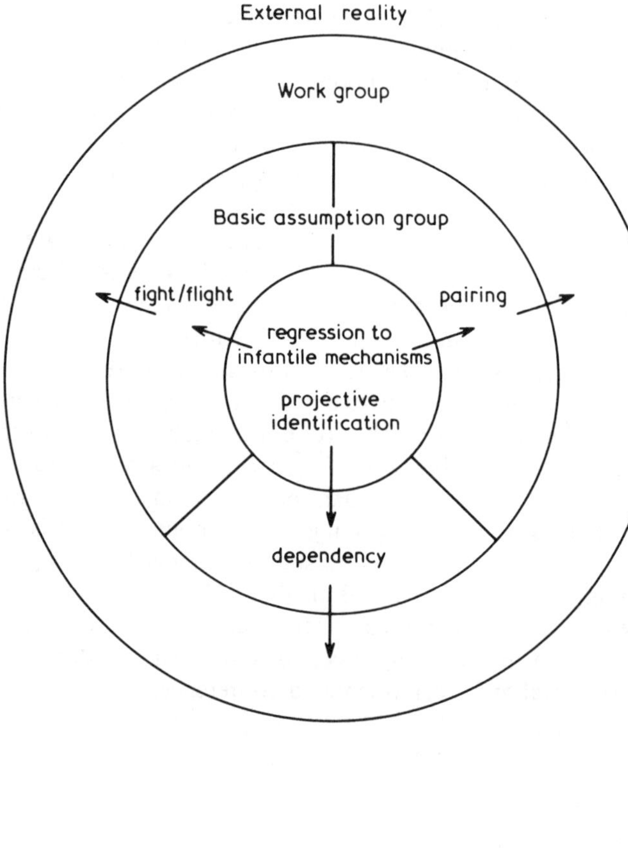

6 The life and work of Kurt Lewin

Any contribution to the study of behaviour in groups and organizations must include the work and influence of Kurt Lewin. Even now the current areas of study in group dynamics (a phrase which he first used) can in most cases be traced back to his original influence. In a memorial address shortly after Lewin's death (1947) Tolman said:

> 'Freud the clinician and Lewin the experimentalist — these are the two men whose names will stand out before all others in the history of our psychological era. For it is their contrasting but complementary insights which first made psychology a science applicable to real human beings and to real human society.' (Marrow 1969: IX)

Although Lewin was a psychologist and not a psychoanalyst, much of his work and many of his ideas are closely related to psychoanalysis. In their article: 'The Relevance of Freudian Psychology and Related Viewpoints for the Social Sciences' Hall and Lindzey wrote:

> 'A few individuals such as Kurt Lewin ... played an important integrative role; within the confines of academic institutions they made earnest efforts to conduct controlled empirical research that was related to, and in part inspired by, psychoanalysis. From these efforts, psychoanalysis received a graver lustre of investigative respectability and this in turn led other more conventional psychologists to conduct related research.' (Hall and Lindzey 1968: 289)

Perhaps, more than most great men, the life of Lewin is as

important as his work, in the sense that his work reflects so greatly his own personal situation and the environment in which he found himself. (See Appendix 1, for a chronological list of Lewin's activities.)

As a German Jew, experiencing anti-semitism in his early academic career (no Jew was likely to become a fully appointed professor in pre-Nazi Germany) and finally forced to flee from the Nazis in 1933, Lewin's work shows a passionate concern for democracy in general and minorities in particular. Even greater than this was his desire to make psychology an applied science, something that would change and improve the social conditions of men and women. Although Lewin propounded many theories he saw them essentially as tools that should be applied to living. 'I am persuaded that scientific sociology and social psychology based on an intimate combination of experiments and empirical theory can do as much or more, for human betterment as the natural sciences have done' (Lewin 1948: 83). This can be summed up in his famous dictum: 'There is nothing so practical as a good theory'.

Lewin's early work in Germany, at the Psychological Institute of Berlin University (1918-33) already revealed his unique approach to psychology. Trained as a psychologist, he had also studied philosophy under Ernst Cassirer and was influenced by the emerging Gestalt psychology, especially by Köhler and Wertheimer who were working in the Institute. During this period Lewin worked with pupils who broke new ground in experimental psychology. The most famous was Bluma Zeigarnick who, as stated earlier, attempted to test Lewin's theory: the desire to carry out a specific task corresponds to the building of a system of psychological tension, and it is the need to discharge this tension that serves to maintain and sustain goal-oriented behaviour until the task is completed. Subjects, both children and adults, were given a series of simple tasks, such as stringing beads, naming cities, and so forth. They were allowed to complete half the tasks and the other half were interrupted before completion. After a time, each subject was asked to recall as many tasks as he could, with the striking result that uncompleted tasks were recalled over completed tasks by a ratio of two to one.

This phenomenon, now called the 'Zeigarnick Effect', demonstrated that undischarged tension or energy was associated with the unfinished tasks and this forced them to be remembered. The energy and tension associated with the completed task had been discharged through carrying out the task and therefore had little remaining power to force it into consciousness. This experiment was important because it was the first experimental confirmation of Lewin's theory of 'psycho dynamics', leading on to his 'field theory', both of which are basic to all his work. His other work at this time was concerned with levels of aspiration, goal achievement, and the genesis of anger.

With the gradual publication of his works and through papers read at international conferences, Lewin's fame began to grow and in 1932 he spent six months at Stanford University as visiting Professor. In 1933, he left Germany for good and after two years at Cornel University, spent the next nine years (1935-44) at the Iowa Child Welfare Research Station. During this time, he attracted many students who wanted to work with him and the list reads like a roll-call of the famous in social psychology: Cartwright, Bavelas, Festinger, Zander, Lippitt, and, although not a psychologist, Mead — the famous anthropologist.

Field theory and life space

The concept of a 'field of forces' originated in physics and refers usually to magnetism or electricity. For instance, the space around a magnet is called the magnetic field, and although invisible, exercises a specific force on an object entering that field. To understand why an electric motor rotates, one has to understand, and mathematically analyse, the forces operating in the magnetic field.

Lewin used this concept of force field to analyse and understand human behaviour. He described it as 'a totality of co-existing facts which are conceived of as mutually interdependent' (Lewin 1972: 200). Each individual exists in a psychological field of forces that, for him, determines and limits his behaviour. This psychological field surrounds each individual and Lewin called this the 'life space'. It is a highly subjective 'space' dealing with the world *as the individual sees it*. Thus, a child's fear of the dark may be dismissed as nonsense by an adult because there is no objective element in it. However, it is real for the child and is very much a part of his psychological field; therefore, it must be taken into account when trying to analyse his behaviour.

Lewin demonstrated the subjective and objective elements in the social field by reference to a married couple. This is illustrated by the following diagram:

Figure 4   Changes in the life space of a husband and wife

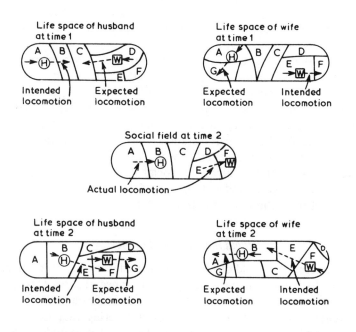

Source: Lewin (1947: II)

At *Time 1*, the husband perceives himself in region *A* and intends to move to region *B*. At the same time, he perceives his wife in region *D* and expects her to move to region *C* (*Figure 4*, upper left). At the same time, the wife sees herself in region *E* and intends to move to *F*. She also perceives her husband to be in region *A* and expects him to move to region *G* (*Figure 4*, upper right). Thus, analysing the two subjective psychological fields of husband and wife provides the basis for predicting the next actual objective piece of behaviour, that is, husband will move to *B* and wife will move to *F* (*Figure 4*, middle).

But what happens next? Both partners are surprised, because neither expected the other to move in the direction they did. The two bottom figures in the diagram illustrate what may happen, with husband and wife again ending up in separate regions. As Lewin says: 'Obviously husband and wife will soon be in trouble if they do not "talk things over", that is, if they do not communicate to each other the structure of their life spaces with the object of equalising them' (Lewin 1947: 12).

In specific terms, the life space for a person will consist of his conscious and unconscious goals, his dreams, hopes, and fears, his past experience and his future expectations. The physical and social conditions will also be important, limiting as they do the variety of possible life spaces and creating the boundary conditions of the psychological field. At the same time, the general background of the situation exerts an influence in the field as a whole, just as the gravitational field exerts an influence in physics. In particular this involves the atmosphere, whether friendly or hostile, and the amount of freedom a person has.

Field theory implies both the concept of dynamic equilibrium and also of reciprocality of movement. Regarding equilibrium it implies that as long as there is no change in the psychological field there will be no change in the person's behaviour (Lewin called this a quasi-stationary equilibrium). However, there may well be tensions. The driving forces and the restraining forces may be equal, but they may be forces of considerable strength. With regard to the reciprocality of movement, this means that any change in the psychological field will result in some change in the person's behaviour and vice versa, a behavioural change must result in a change in the field.

Field theory and group behaviour

The implications of these ideas were clearly seen by Lewin, especially in relation to behaviour in a group. According to the culture, or group atmosphere, the individual's level of conduct (L^P) may differ from the level of the group standards (L^{GR}) by a permitted amount n, that is, $L^{GR} - L^P = n$.

The group standard has a social attraction for the individual's behaviour. In Lewin's terms, it has a positive valence. Thus, the individual's behaviour will change largely as a result of change in the group standards, that is, for any change in L^{GR}, there will tend to be a similar change in L^P in order to preserve the value of n.

This theory was shown to be true in several experiments that Lewin initiated, designed to change food and feeding habits. They were concerned with persuading people to change from buying expensive cuts of meat to eating offal and so forth, and with persuading mothers to give fresh milk and orange juice to their babies. In all cases, two different methods of influence were used. In the first instance, the information was given by lectures and individual instructions with menu and diet sheets. In the second method a step-by-step group discussion was used resulting in a self-attained group decision.

After two weeks, a significant difference was found in the percentage of people who had actually changed their behaviour. For instance, almost 90 per cent of the mothers involved in the group decision were giving orange juice compared with only 40 per cent who had received individual instructions. An even more significant result emerged after four weeks when it was discovered that 100 per cent of the group decision mothers were responding. Lewin said:

> 'If resistance to change depends partly on the value of the group standard for the individual, the resistance to change should be diminished if one uses a procedure which diminished the strength of the value of the group standard or which changes the level that is perceived by the individual as having social value... If the group standard itself is changed, the resistance which is due to the relation between individual and group standard is eliminated.'   (Lewin 1947: 34)

This led Lewin to generalize the process of change in the group in terms of three steps:

(a) Unfreezing — this first step involves a reappraisal of old values and requires a willingness to have an open mind that will, perhaps for the first time, consider disconfirming data. Different problems will require different approaches but 'to break open the shell of complacency and self-righteousness, it is sometimes necessary to bring about deliberately an emotional stir-up.' (Lewin 1947: 35)

(b) Moving — this involves actually performing the new behaviour.

(c) Freezing — the group now maintains its new level. Lewin

said that this comes from two forces. One is the individual's tendency to stick to his decision. The other is due to the commitment to the group. This was true even in the 'orange juice' situation where decisions made in a group setting continued to influence individual behaviour, even though the individuals did not meet each other again.

The 'field at a given time'

Lewin's field theory has been criticized and frequently misunderstood in relation to the way he deals with time and past events. One of his basic statements about the psychological field theory is that 'Any behaviour or any other change in a psychological field depends only upon the psychological field *at that time*' (Lewin 1952: 45). This has led people to think that Lewin disregarded the past as having no importance in the analysis and description of current behaviour. Nevertheless, in various papers, he made it quite clear that this is not what he said. In essence, Lewin stated that past experience is relevant to current behaviour, but only in so far as it exerts an influence in the field currently in the 'here and now'. In a person's life space, the psychological past, the psychological present, and the psychological future are highly significant. One of the differences between the child and the adult is the higher degree of differentiation in the latter, especially regarding this psychological time perspective. This is shown in *Figure 5* (see over) which also contains Lewin's concept of 'irreality' — that seems very similar to the Freudian concept of phantasy. The adult, in contrast to the child, has not only a longer past available for recall but is also able to imagine a more distant future. The adult's behaviour should reflect a greater degree of possible courses of action than the child's, because of these psychological influences.

Lewin was keen to use mathematics to illustrate his ideas of psychological forces in the same way that they are used in physics to describe physical events, and he attempted to apply mathematics to his concept of 'the field at a given time'.

If dx is a differential change in x during a differential time period dt, then the change $\frac{dx}{dt}$ at time t depends only on the situation s^t at that time: $\frac{dx}{dt} = F(s^t)$

The equivalent to $\frac{dx}{dt}$ in physics is the concept of 'behaviour' in psychology. Therefore behaviour b at the time t is a function

Figure 5   The life space at two developmental stages

Stage a

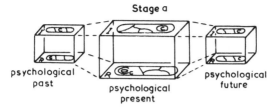

psychological
past

psychological
present

psychological
future

Stage b

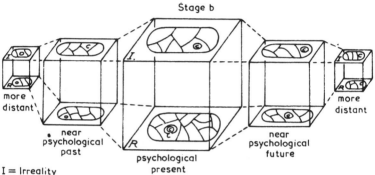

more
distant

near
psychological
past

psychological
present

near
psychological
future

more
distant

I = Irreality
R = Reality

Source: Lewin (1972: 203)

of the situation at time t only: $b^t = F(s^t)$

Lewin revealed and used this principle of contemporaneity in a discussion of psychological regression. Freud had used the concept of regression to describe mainly adult sexual behaviour when it exhibits characteristics of an earlier childhood pattern. He saw mature sexuality as a steady progression in libidinal interest and activity from oral to anal and finally to full genitality. Regression occurs when the libido turns back 'like a wanderer in a new region who falls back to earlier camps when he encounters obstacles'.

Lewin questioned this description from a dynamic standpoint. Time cannot turn back so, in that sense, the libido cannot turn back. To represent regression in terms of field theory requires a 'here and now' statement and diagram that illustrates the forces operating in the person's life space at any given time. The following diagram shows the way in which Lewin solved this problem.

Figure 6   Field representing the conditions of regression (according to Freud's substitute theory of regression)

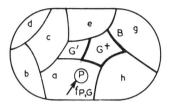

P = person; G^+ = original goal; G' = substitute goal to which the subject regresses; B = obstacle between P and G^+ (barrier); a,b,c, ... regions of the life space; fP,G = force of the direction of the goal.

Source: Lewin (1952: 92)

The person *P* tries to reach the goal G^+, that in this case, represents a need characteristic of a certain level of maturity. However, this goal is not accessible at the present time, due to the boundary *B*. Under these conditions, the person turns to another goal *G'* that represents less mature behaviour. Although *G'* is different from G^+, nevertheless it offers at least some satisfaction and enables *P* to release some of the tension caused by the force *fPG*, that is, he regresses. Lewin says:

'At the moment, it is not important to discuss whether this theory is right or wrong. It will suffice to say that this is essentially a field theory. It is an attempt to characterise the situation at a given time and to make the topology of the life space and certain dynamic properties of its regions (attractiveness, barrier, etc.) responsible for a certain event.'

(Lewin 1952: 92)

Topology and Mathematics

In 1936 Lewin published *Principles of Topological Psychology* in which he showed how the branch of geometry, called topology, could be used to give a more precise representation of behaviour. His twin hopes were first, that this approach would provide a common language for psychologists, irrespective of their particular schools of thought, and second, that it would make psychology more scientific. Basically, it involves drawing a lozenge shape figure to represent a person's life space and within this, representing the various regions within this field, together with the operative forces and available goals. *Figures 4* and *6* are good examples of this approach. With regard to his use of mathematics, he used it in a highly representative manner, never using numbers or quantities. As a result, no matter how Lewin's mathematical symbols are manipulated, they never generate new knowledge. Like chess pieces on a board, Lewin moved them around in new and interesting combinations, but in the end they remain unproductive symbols. From a mathematical viewpoint topology is rather primitive. Cartwright observed 'Lewin's attitude towards mathematics displayed a strong ambivalence; he was attracted by its rigour but fearful of what he called premature formalization' (Marrow 1969: 80). While Lewin's influence has been enormous, it seems that topological psychology and his idiosyncratic use of mathematics has not continued after his death.

Practical research

By 1940 Lewin was regarded as one of the leading experimental and theoretical psychologists in the United States. His fame rested not only on the experimental results he obtained, but also on the breadth of his imagination and interest. During his period at Iowa, three significant pieces of original work were carried out that are still highly relevant to the general study of social psychology today, and that also reveal this breadth of interest.

Frustration and regression

This experiment was a continuation of the work started in Berlin and included a colleague from that time, Tamara Dembo (Barker, Dembo, and Lewin 1941). Briefly, five-year-olds were observed at normal play and then they were deliberately frustrated. The period of play following frustration was then observed and compared with the first period and rated for constructiveness. The overall conclusion was that frustration resulted in a regression in the level of intellectual functioning, increased unhappiness, restlessness, and destructiveness. These results confirmed Lewin's initial hypothesis that frustration affects both intellectual and emotional behaviour.

Autocracy-democracy studies

These studies of behaviour were carried out with groups of boys in hobby clubs and observed the effect of different styles of leadership — autocratic, democratic, and laissez-faire. (See p. 10 for more details.) Lewin, in his original article, summed up the results in the following manner:

(i) In the first experiment hostility was thirty times as frequent in the autocratic as in the democratic group. Aggression was eight times as frequent, with much aggression directed towards two successive scapegoats. (Significantly, this aggression was not projected into the source of their feelings, that is, the autocratic leader, but into fellow members.)

(ii) In the second experiment, a new category of leadership was introduced, laissez-faire, and it was this type that caused most aggression. In the autocratic group an extremely non-aggressive, apathetic pattern of behaviour evolved.

(iii) This lack of aggression was caused by the repressive behaviour of the autocrat as demonstrated by a sharp rise of aggression that occurred when the autocrat left the room. Nineteen, out of the twenty boys liked the democratic leader better than the autocratic leader.

Lewin considered these results to be highly significant and frequently referred to them in other articles. Not only did they provide scientific evidence for the superiority of democracy in which he passionately believed, but they also showed that the social climate is not an intangible concept but a psychological reality whose effect can be studied. Referring to these experiments, he said: 'Psychological atmospheres are empirical realities and are scientifically describable facts' (Lewin 1972: 201).

Action research in industry

The third important piece of work involved Lewin in the practical and high pressure world of American mass production industry. He had already published a paper in 1920 concerning Taylor's system of 'scientific management' in which Lewin said that work has a 'life-value' and that every job should sustain or enhance this. Prophetically he said that the task of making jobs richer and more satisfying is a job not only for the efficiency expert, but also for the research psychologist. In 1939 he had the opportunity to put his ideas into practice in the Harwood manufacturing company. This company, producing pyjamas (later to be immortalized in the musical *The Pyjama Game*) in the industrialized north, had established a factory in the rural small town of Marion, Virginia. The new employees were mainly young women who, after twelve weeks of training, were only achieving about half the production achieved in the northern plant.

Lewin made a number of visits to the company and then, influenced by the earlier food-habit experiments and the autocracy-democracy studies, he encouraged Bavelas to start an experimental study of human factors in factory management.

Bavelas worked in the area of groups and showed how group decisions could improve output and productivity. One of the most interesting experiments concerned the use of 'pacing cards', by which a small group of workers planned their own hourly pace by means of such cards. The production level rose from sixty-seven units to eighty-two units and stabilized itself at this level, while the control group remained unchanged (Lewin 1947).

After Lewin's death, further experiments were carried out by French and Coch (Coch was the personnel manager). One of their important findings was concerned with overcoming resistance to change. Owing to market changes, production needs required that operators should be transferred from old jobs to new ones, and this involved considerable time being spent in retraining. Naturally the women resisted these transfers, and this resulted in low morale and output. Coch and French devised an experiment in which these transfers were handled in three different ways.

In the first variation, the control group involved no participation by employees, who were simply informed of the changes, although they were given an explanation. In the second variation, there was participation in the changes through the workers' representatives. In the third variation, there was total participation of all the group members in designing the change.

The results, measured over thirty days, were striking. In the no-participation group, there were expressions of resistance and hostility, deliberate restriction of output, and most significantly,

17 per cent of the group left. In the participation-through-representatives group, there were good and co-operative relationships, and within fourteen days they had achieved their original output level. However, in the total-participation group, efficiency ratings returned to the pre-change level after only two days and then climbed steadily until they reached and maintained a level 14 per cent higher than the pre-change level (Coch and French 1948: 522, *figure 4*).

All these results were interpreted in terms of Lewin's theory of psycho dynamics. Production level represents the quasi-stationary equilibrium resulting from driving and restraining forces in the work situation. This level can be changed in two ways, either by increasing the driving forces or by decreasing the restraining forces. Lewin argued that attempts to raise production levels by increasing the driving forces increases tension and 'since increase of tension above a certain degree goes parallel with greater fatigue, higher aggressiveness, higher emotionality and lower constructiveness it is clear that as a rule the second method [i.e. reduction of the restraining forces] will be preferable to the high pressure method' (Lewin 1947: 26).

The total-participation method not only reduced the restraining forces but also helped the group to 'freeze' at a permanently higher level of output.

Social issues

In 1944 Lewin left Iowa and moved to the Massachusetts Institute of Technology, where he set up the Research Centre for Group Dynamics. This new project represented a development in Lewin's thought and work, for after the early 1940s he published very little that was new concerning the 'person'. He became more and more interested in groups of all kinds — family, work, religious, and community — and was concerned to build up a body of knowledge and a general theory about groups. In an article published in 1939, 'Experiments in Social Space' (where he first used the term 'group dynamics'), Lewin made explicit his belief that, in the right environment, the social scientist could make a real contribution to society's improvement and welfare. Yet he was sufficiently a realist to know that progress in this area was not inevitable. 'The development of such a realistic, non-mystical, social science and the possibility of its fruitful application presupposes the existence of a society which believes in reason' (Lewin 1948: 83).

At the Centre for Group Dynamics, Lewin rapidly built up a team of colleagues who had been working with him over the years, including Radke, Festinger, Lippitt, and Cartwright. He also worked closely with other eminent social scientists including McGregor and Allport. Lewin's influence was enormous, both on his colleagues and on the many doctoral students who came to study under him. In this period, over 125 papers were published and this total is probably unprecedented among any group of psychologists.

Lewin's constant concerns were democracy, the Jews, and minority groups and in 1944 he launched the Commission on Community Interrelations, a body sponsored by the American Jewish Congress. This commission was set up to carry out an action-research programme to discover, and then overcome, the forces leading to anti-semitism in every aspect of social life, and problems facing other minorities including non-Jew, white, and negro. The commission was soon involved in such things as the employment of negroes on sales counters, gang fights between Jews and non-Jews, and integrated housing. One of their notable successes was the challenging of the *numerus clauses* in American colleges and universities that set a level on the number of Jewish students who could be enrolled. A successful law suit against the medical school of Columbia University, although settled out of court, started the gradual erosion of this particular kind of minority discrimination.

Sensitivity training — the origin of the T-group

As though by accident the various strands of Lewin's work were about to coalesce and produce an innovation in education and learning that has made a tremendous impact on most social institutions not only in America but also in many other countries as well. In 1946, he was asked to organize and direct a conference to help train leaders and conduct research on the most effective means of combating racial and religious prejudice. The conference took place in Connecticut and the participants were mainly teachers and social workers, a few labour leaders and business men, and about half were Negroes and Jews. Benne, Bradford, and Lippitt were the training leaders, and Lewin led the team of researchers. The members worked in three groups of ten, and the work was carried out mainly through group discussions and role plays in an attempt to analyse and understand the various social problems with which they were concerned. In the evenings, most of the members went home, but the staff held a meeting to analyse and discuss the data that they had collected in their observations of the three groups during the day. Some participants living on the campus asked if they might sit in on these staff discussions. The result was electrifying as they heard, and then reacted to, a discussion about their own behaviour.

'To the training staff it seemed that a potentially powerful medium and process of re-education had been, somewhat inadvertently, hit upon. Group members, if they were confronted more or less objectively with data concerning their own behavior and its effects, and if they came to participate nondefensively in thinking about these data, might achieve highly meaningful learnings about themselves, about the responses of others to them, and about group behavior and group development in general. At this time, no thought was given to the exclusion of other content, whether in the form of cases suggested by staff, situations reported by members from outside the group, or of role-played incidents. Initially, the notion was to supplement this there-and-then content with the collection and analysis of here-and-now data concerning the members' own behaviors.'

(Bradford, Gibb, and Benne 1964: 83)

After six months, the participants were surveyed to see the extent to which they were able to use their new-found skills and insights in their work in the community. Seventy-five per cent declared that they were now more skilful in improving group relations and they all spoke about their increased sensitivity to the feelings of others.

Following the discovery of this training method, involving feedback about behaviour, the National Training Laboratories were established the following year at Gould Academy, Bethel, and a workshop was organized which incorporated some of the Connecticut procedures. One of the features of this workshop was a small, ongoing group called the Basic Skills Training Group, where behavioural data collected from observation was made available for discussion and analysis by the group. This method of education and training is now universally known as 'T-group' training.

Lewin died in 1947 just before the first Bethel conference took place, but it left him a continuing memorial. The National Training Laboratories continue to this day as one of the world centres of practice and research in the field of T-group training and group dynamics. Since then, there has been an extraordinary growth of training and encounter groups, and no matter how different and varied they have now become, they all involve Lewin's concept of observing 'here and now' data, analysing it, and using feedback among the members in order to develop their social and interpersonal skills.

Another enduring memorial to Lewin is the learned journal *Human Relations.* At the Tavistock Institute of Human Relations in London, Trist and Wilson wrote to Lewin asking him if he would consider establishing the journal jointly, that is, between the Tavistock Institute and Lewin's Centre for Group Dynamics at Massachusetts Institute of Technology. Lewin agreed and the first issue in June 1947 (published after his death) commenced with his article 'Frontiers in Group Dynamics'.

7   T-groups and the laboratory method of learning

Since 1947 T-groups and the laboratory method have rapidly become major educational methods in many Western countries and continue to be widely used, especially in managerial training and organizational development. Part of this popularity is due to the ethical beliefs embedded in the method that reflect aspects of American culture concerning democracy and democratic leadership, and the way in which people ought to relate to one another. As Bradford, Gibb, and Benne (who were all Fellows of the National Training Laboratories at Bethel) wrote: 'The T-group is more than an educational technology. It has its roots in a system of values relative to mature, productive and right relationships among people. It is grounded in assumptions about human nature, human learning and human change' (Bradford, Gibb, and Benne 1964: 1).

This chapter attempts to clarify the nature and purpose of T-groups and aims especially to:

- (i) Define the purpose of a T-group.
- (ii) Describe what happens in a T-group.
- (iii) Examine a model of the stages of development in a group.
- (iv) Consider some evidence regarding the power of T-groups to affect behaviour.
- (v) To examine in detail one particular model of a T-group, namely the Leicester/Tavistock Conference, both from the literature and from the author's personal experience.

What is the purpose of a T-group?

There can be no single answer to this question, just as, for instance, there can be no single answer to the question: 'What is the purpose of a university?' However, the purpose of a T-group involves the development of human skills of behaviour and the understanding of the processes of human relations. T-groups are essentially controlled instruments of change providing opportunities for self-knowledge and self-development, and their effectiveness is measured by an increase in those areas of personal behaviour judged to be important. These are usually taken to include an increase in self-awareness and in the perception of the effect that one's behaviour has on another. Peter Smith said that T-group training has three principal goals (Smith 1969: iii):

(a) To increase the ability to appreciate how others are reacting to one's own behaviour.
(b) To increase the ability to gauge the state of relationships between others.
(c) To increase the ability to carry out skilfully the behaviour required by the situation.

These aims can be illustrated by means of a diagram called the 'Johari Window' (so-called because it was developed by two psychologists Joe Luft and Harry Ingham).

The diagram shows three categories of behaviour, 'public', 'blind', and 'hidden'. Behaviour that can be described as 'public' is perceived and known both by the individual and by everyone else. 'Blind' behaviour describes those actions and manners of behaviour that have an effect on others but of which the individual is unaware. 'Hidden' behaviour refers to facts, emotions, and feelings that an individual is aware of, but that he deliberately chooses not to share with anyone else. The shaded area in the bottom right-hand corner is both blind and hidden and is usually referred to as the 'unconscious'. Smith claimed that it is not part of the task of the T-group to explore the unconscious, but many would disagree with this statement.

The aim of the T-group is to help individuals realize and understand (sometimes for the first time) these various aspects of their behaviour and then to make changes if they so choose. In Lewin's terms (see p. 54) the boundaries of their behaviour are, first, unfrozen; second, the individual receives new knowledge and insights and may choose to incorporate them into his behaviour; and third, these new boundaries are 'refrozen'.

Figure 7   Johari window

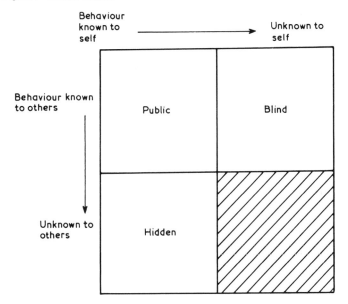

Source: Smith (1969: 2)

The process at work in a T-group is one of learning and it can
be argued that the only proof that something has been learnt is if
it results in a change in behaviour. In a T-group, a member is able
to use each other member as a mirror of his own behaviour,
through the process of feedback. He may choose to ignore this
information but, for instance, if the rest of the group indicate
authentically, that is, without ulterior motives, that his behaviour
has a particular effect on them, commonsense indicates that he
will do well to take notice of this. However, within this process
lies both the strength and the weakness of this form of learning.
The strength is that new knowledge about oneself can be achieved
(it can be argued that for many people a T-group provides a
unique opportunity for such frank and honest information) and
can result in genuine growth and development of the person. The
weakness is that the process involves emotions and feelings that
can be extremely painful when past behaviour is analysed and new
ways of behaving are considered.

How much pain, in the sense of experiencing anxiety and other unpleasant emotions an individual should undergo, and for how long, is a very controversial topic. The strain of exam preparation and then the actual taking of them, either at school or university spread over a three or four year period, is accepted as an essential part of the academic learning process. However, learning about oneself, in the way provided by T-groups, concentrates the learning and change process into a short period; therefore strain, anxiety, and strong emotions will be experienced sharply. A later section will analyse the evidence concerning the damage, if any, which a person can suffer through this method of 'education'.

The purpose of a T-group can include aims other than the three given by Smith. The T-group is usually only a part of a conference or training programme that uses the laboratory method to provide learning about other aspects of behaviour. For instance, the course or conference can itself be regarded as a temporary system of organization and it can itself be studied in the 'here and now' in order to provide knowledge about organizational behaviour. The manner in which groups interact, the way in which one group will attempt to meet its own needs, and the conflicting needs of the total conference are experiences that have obvious parallels with departmental behaviour in commercial and industrial organizations.

In fact, T-groups are often used for management training and development, because they create situations in which the essential elements of managerial activity and organizational life are highlighted. The issues of authority, leadership, and co-operation together with those of roles, task, and standards are of equal importance to those of individual behaviour and interaction and have their obvious counterpart in industry and commerce.

What happens in a T-group?

A T-group usually consists of between seven and ten people with a tutor or trainer, and it usually sits in a circle. The essential method of operation is the study of the behaviour of the group as it happens in the 'here and now'. No formal structure is given to the group, so that members may sit where they choose and may discuss any topic or issue. Members are also free to start or join in a discussion or abstain from the debate, and they are free to use any style of behaviour they select. Central to this activity is the trainer, whose job is to assist the group to understand what is actually happening and to learn from this. While in practice different trainers use different approaches, there is a commonality in what they do and, equally important, in what they abstain from doing.

They draw attention to what is going on, but they do not judge this activity. They help the group to ask the appropriate questions but they do not give the answers. While they will speak openly and frankly about relationships in the group, they themselves will not form a special relationship with any group member. They will continually try to construct a learning situation but they will not teach. They provide a focus for concerns, both real and imaginary, about authority and authority figures, but at the same time they will act in a non-authoritarian manner.

T-group meetings commence and end at precisely defined times. Even though the group may be in full swing, the trainer may leave at the appointed time, which allows the group to learn about boundaries and the constraints that time puts on all activities, especially in an organizational setting.

A T-group provides a new social situation which requires each member to reconsider his usual behaviour and attitudes in order to discover what is appropriate and effective in this new culture. Whitman put this well:

'Just as the infant must be socialised from the very beginning of his life as if there had not been 5000 years of culture before him, so must the (T) group, in a vastly attenuated form, find its own culture and laws from the beginning. While each group member, as an adult, shares an approximately equal cultural background, each must experience every other as an essentially new entity. The group forms its own history and constructs its own standards and modes of behaviour and, once fixed, they are extremely difficult to alter.' (Whitman 1964: 315)

It is this process of reconsideration and revaluation, together with unbiased and honest information about himself, that can result in the individual changing his behaviour. The learning results from living through new and powerful experiences that involve encountering people in a low-risk situation. Consequently, the lessons that an individual learns in a T-group about himself and his effect on others are not remembered in the same way in which facts and figures are memorized. Rather, they become internalized and integrated into his ongoing behaviour, in the same way in which a child's early experiences automatically affect and modify his future actions.

A model of development in a T-group

Every T-group will be unique in terms of the behaviour that occurs within the group and the learning that is achieved by individual members. T-groups will have different objectives and each trainer will have a different approach. However, having made these provisos, it should be possible to describe those developments and patterns that are common to any T-group. Bennis has made one of the most useful attempts to do this and the following is a description of his theory (Bennis 1964).

The behaviour generated in a T-group arises from the way in which the group responds to its unsolved problems. In terms of the individual member, there are two areas of internal uncertainty. One is the area concerning dependence and his relationship with authority and authority figures. The second has to do with interdependence and how he forms and deals with personal relationships.

Concerning the first area of dependence, there are people in the group who are at the very 'dependent' end of the scale. They need and find comfort in such things as rules and agenda and wish to rely on 'experts'. At the opposite end are those who are 'counter-dependent' and who are discomforted by authority. People who are at either end of the scale, that is, dependent or counter-dependent, are said to be 'conflicted' in that they show compulsiveness towards either extreme and this must result in some internal conflict that will be revealed in the group.

Concerning the second area of interdependency, a similar scale can be used to describe group members' behaviour regarding personal relationships. At one end are those who are 'over-personal' and feel they must establish and maintain a high degree of intimacy. At the opposite end are those who tend to avoid intimacy and are described as 'counter-personal'. Again, those group members who have a compulsion to be at either end of the scale are 'conflicted'.

However, important to the life of the group are those

'unconflicted' members, who have no compulsion to be at any of the extremes, either concerning dependency or interdependency, and it is these 'independent' members of the group who frequently help the group to move to the next useful phase.

Bennis then built on these ideas and used them to describe the phases in the development of the T-group:

Phase I — Dependence

    Subphase 1 Dependence — flight
    Subphase 2 Counter-dependence — fight
    Subphase 3 Resolution — catharsis.

Phase II — Interdependence

    Subphase 4 Enchantment — flight
    Subphase 5 Disenchantment — fight
    Subphase 6 Consensual validation

Phase I

Subphase 1 *Dependence — flight*: When the group commences, the main feeling among the group members is anxiety as they search for group goals and significant roles. Most of the behaviour exhibited will be that which has gained approval from authority figures in the past. Nevertheless, underlying all this is the common feeling in the group that the trainer is not telling them what they should do.

Subphase 2 *Counter-dependence — fight*: The group now feel that the trainer has failed them miserably and therefore they become counter-dependent. Subgroups may emerge and the trainer is likely to be either bullied or ignored. Yet there is always the secret hope in the group that this chaos, together with the very unpleasant feelings generated, is part of the master plan, that is, the failure may be theirs and not his.

Subphase 3 *Resolution — catharsis*: This is the most crucial and fragile phase, but its positive elements arise from the preceding subphases 1 and 2. During those times, some bonds of mutual support have developed and the trainer's words have made an impact. The independent members play a strong role and, at last, the group is able to openly discuss and challenge the trainer's role and authority. The outcome is that the group achieves autonomy.

Phase II

Subphase 4 *Enchantment — flight*: The resolution of the authority problem gives the group a feeling of euphoria. Initially all is sweetness and light with the myth of universal harmony, but gradually unease sets in as rigid norms are set which attempt to prevent anything from destroying this apparent group harmony.

Subphase 5 *Disenchantment — fight*: The group now tends to subdivide into the 'over-personals' and the 'counter-personals', that is, those who want complete intimacy and those who reject this. Probably all share the feeling that intimacy breeds contempt, and the anxiety arises from each individual feeling that he might be rejected if his true self was actually revealed. This phase is frequently revealed by absenteeism and boredom.

Subphase 6 *Consensual validation*: Because, among other things, the end of the group is approaching, there are strong pressures on the group to resolve the interdependency problem. There is a need to establish a method of role evaluation and (as in subphase 3) the 'independent' member can cut through the group's fears by a request for an evaluation of his role. When this happens, the fears of rejection are diminished when tested against reality. Members can then accept one another's differences without categorizing them as either good or bad, and genuine understanding and communication can take place.

This description of the phases in the development of a T-group requires qualification. No group will exhibit these phases in such a clearly observable manner. Bennis said:

'Life in a T-group is more of a "puzzlement" than any such simple classification suggests. Rather than the thesis-antithesis-synthesis dialectic presented here, where one phase movement chronologically follows another and inexorably erases all traces of the past, the process more closely resembles a cyclical movement where the major problems evolve at different points in time — the groups attempting a deeper understanding each time around.'   (Bennis 1964: 269)

What is the effect of a T-group on behaviour?

It is notoriously difficult to measure the effectiveness of

educational methods. This is especially true of T-groups because this method operates in the emotional and imprecise area of human relations. In particular what may seem to be a significant change to the individual may appear trivial and even banal to someone else. Many surveys have attempted to measure the feelings of participants after attending a T-group, but by its very nature, the results are highly subjective. Bunker carried out an evaluation of T-group training by surveying over 200 people some time after they had attended courses at the National Training Laboratories, including the reactions and views of people who had worked with them (Bunker 1965). In comparing these findings with a control group, the overall results showed that significant changes had occurred in the experimental subjects. These changes were especially apparent in such behavioural areas as the ability to relate to others, increased interdependence, a greater acceptance of others, and a greater insight into self and role.

Campbell and Dunnette surveyed the evaluation studies of T-groups used in management training and development (Campbell and Dunnette 1968). They concluded that the evidence is 'reasonably convincing' that T-group training does induce behavioural changes in the 'back-home' situation. However, they found no conclusive data that specified the nature of these changes. They also mentioned a large number of results based on 'internal data', that is, people's own description of self-perceived changes that, from a scientific standpoint, shows that they now use more interpersonal-type words, but does not reveal the accuracy of these self-perceptions.

In a study published in 1977, Cooper examined the small group training programmes run by five training and management consultancy organizations in the United Kingdom which involved 227 managers. His overall findings concerning the positive effects of group training reveal that in terms of personality changes, participants generally became 'emotionally more stable', more 'trusting and adaptable', more 'humble and mild', but also more 'restrained and timid'. Most significantly although up to six weeks after training no meaningful changes in work or family relationships appeared, after seven months these trainees were seen by work colleagues as significantly improving their work relationships and by their friends and relatives as 'coping better with difficult family and personal matters'. On an individual basis sixty-two participants (30 per cent) showed at least one significant positive change (on corroborative evidence) after six weeks and fifty four (24 per cent) showed at least one significant positive change after seven months.

Resulting from the unprecedented growth of this method of education (which has sometimes been used with more enthusiasm than skill), T-groups and the laboratory method are popularly seen either as the best innovation in the whole area of learning and change or else as a harmful method, used by imposters that can cause irreparable damage to the human psyche. Lakin said:

> 'Twenty-two years after its beginnings, in the wake of the most spectacular period of growth in popularity and interest, it is hard to know what is more dangerous for the future of the training movement: its over-enthusiastic and uncritical adherents and supporters or increasingly agitated critics. Training is under attack by some for being a gigantic hoax in which nothing of value occurs. By others it is believed that significant damage is done to individuals and organizations.'
>
> (Lakin 1972: 161)

Cooper surveyed the literature concerning the psychological dangers of T-group training (Cooper 1975). One of the more scientific studies quoted was carried out by Ross, Kligfield, and Whitman (1971) and involved the city of Cincinnati where almost 3,000 people had attended T-group training over a period of five years. By contacting all the psychiatrists in the area, they discovered the number of people whose mental illness had derived from these experiences. This convincing study showed that those people brought to psychiatric attention represented 0.66 per cent of the population thought to be at risk because of attending T-groups. Cooper's own studies on English students attending groups revealed no adverse symptoms but showed some evidence that, as a result, they were better able to withstand stress, in this case the stress of final examinations at a university.

In his 1977 study of T-group attendance (mentioned on p. 73) Cooper found that 5 per cent of the participants sampled were identified as having had a potentially negative experience on a short-term basis (up to six weeks after training). However, out of this 5 per cent (twelve managers) originally designated as potentially 'hurt' by their T-group experience at six weeks, seven showed marked significant improvements at seven months when judged by corroborative evidence. Cooper says: 'It might be argued, therefore, that in the short term some kind of emotional reaction may be, for a small number of participants, a necessary precondition to long term change' (Cooper 1977: 24). It is interesting to compare that statement with Lewin's, when he was describing the process of change in terms of 'unfreezing'. 'To break open the shell of complacency and self-righteousness, it is sometimes necessary to bring about deliberately an emotional stir-up' (Lewin 1947: 35).

The Tavistock conferences at Leicester

In 1957 a conference was organized jointly by Leicester University and the Tavistock Institute of Human Relations that was the first full-scale experiment to use the laboratory method of training in Britain.*

The conference was strongly influenced by the work of the National Training Laboratories at Bethel, United States, where the laboratory training method involving T-groups had been used since 1948. In that year, two British social scientists, both psychoanalysts, had been members of the National Training Laboratories staff and in 1955 and 1956 some seminars had been organized in London sponsored by the British Institute of Management and the Industrial Welfare Society (of which Rice had been Deputy Director), together with the help of American consultants. Following this work, the Tavistock Institute and Clinic were asked by several industrial organizations to conduct similar courses for executives and training officers. Forty-five members attended the Leicester conference, half coming from industry and commerce, and the remainder from education, the social services, and the prison and probation service. The conference lasted for two weeks and on most days there was a 'study group' that was similar to the American T-group, and in which there was a consultant and an observer. The task of the study group members was to examine their own behaviour in the 'here and now' and to observe their development over the period of the conference. These study groups formed the core experience of the conference and although the consultants differed from one

*Trist and Sofer (1959) gives a full report of the first conference.

another in their individual approach, they had all been influenced by the ideas of Bion. There were also application groups, theory sessions, and visits to outside organizations such as the local prison and the education authority.

A second conference was held in 1959 and since then one, and latterly two, conferences have been held annually. Changes and innovations have been made. From 1962 to 1968 Rice directed all the Leicester Tavistock Conferences and under his influence the conference shifted its emphasis. Writing in 1965 about his experiences of directing these conferences he said: 'I am now working on the assumption that the primary task of the residential conferences with which my colleagues and I are concerned is to provide those who attend with opportunities to learn about leadership' (Rice 1965: 5). Since then, the emphasis has moved and the brochure for the September 1976 conference was entitled *Authority, Leadership and Organisation*. It stated that the primary task was 'to provide members with the opportunities to learn about the nature of authority and the inter-personal, inter-group and institutional problems encountered in exercising it within the Conference organisation'.

Method and content of the Tavistock conferences

The method and content of these conferences has changed considerably from the original format. The major difference is that there is now no didactic teaching. On the first conference, 23 per cent of the content was occupied by theory and lecture sessions, but in current courses the whole event is concerned with experiential learning.

Table 1 shows an analysis of the content of five conferences over the last twenty years.

The main work of the conference now consists of four events which are (a) small groups, (b) large group, (c) the intergroup event, and (d) application groups.

(*a*) *Small groups.* The small groups consist of eight to twelve people and are equivalent to the T-group. Their aim is to allow the members to study and explore their own behaviour as it arises in the 'here and now'. Each group has a consultant to help it in this task. The influence of Bion is very evident in the method used by

Table 1 *Content analysis of Tavistock conferences (%)*

Activities	1957 (1st)	1964	1972	1975	1976
Large group	–	15	22	20	14
Study group/small group	30	29	25	24	31
Intergroup event	–	13	14	8	14
Review group	–	–	10	7	10
Application group	16	17	8	8	8
Institutional event	–	–	14	20	14
Plenaries	9	9	7	13	9
Theory/lecture sessions	23	17	–	–	–
Films	4	–	–	–	–
Special activities	9	–	–	–	–
Other events	9	–	–	–	–

the consultants, who interpret group behaviour as a whole, seeing group processes as unconscious collusion between members through projective identification and other defence mechanisms described by Klein. In all the events, the staff play a particular role that allows members to project on to them their unconscious feelings concerning authority figures and then attempt to resolve and understand them.

Such a situation inevitably provokes strong emotions including members' hostility to their consultant. Unconsciously they would sooner learn about other people than themselves. The situation also implies that they may have failed to do this in the past and therefore the work of the group can be experienced as an affront to their self-respect. In all this, the consultant's job (as Rice put it) is:

> 'to confront the group without affronting its members; to draw attention to group behaviour and not to individual behaviour; to point out how the group uses individuals to express its own emotions; how it exploits some members so that others can absolve themselves from the responsibility for such expression.' (Rice 1965: 65)

In Bion's terms, the role of the consultant is to act as leader of the work group, to refuse to occupy a leadership role in any of the basic assumption groups, and to assist the group to understand when it is working in such a mode. These small groups end a day or so before the end of the conference, so that any comfort or security gained in them can be tested against reality.

(*b*)   *The large group.*   This exercise was introduced by Rice and is now a central part of the conference. It consists of all the members (usually between sixty to seventy) together with the consultants, meeting in a large group where 'in the crowd-like setting, amidst the rapid emergence of groups and anti-groups and the development of myths, the individual may feel at times that his conceptions of himself and the situation are often unsupported' (Tavistock Institute of Human Relations 1976: 3).

The large group in particular reveals the process of projective identification and the formation of the three basic assumption modes of working. Turquet, who was for many years a consultant to the large group at these conferences, said that the major anxiety experienced by members concerned the threat to their identity. The constant need of the individual member in the large group is to find a role and to retain it throughout the life of the large group. However, because of its size, the group is in a constant state of flux and the individual experiences the very strong forces which emanate from all the members. In this constantly changing situation, the individual rarely, if ever, experiences a state of equilibrium as roles, with all their accompanying emotions and assumptions, are rapidly projected, and as rapidly withdrawn. Describing this, Turquet wrote: 'In the harsh terms of group life, it is a case of who will dominate whom: will consultant and member dominate the large group or be dominated by it?' (Turquet 1975: 92). The individual member can avoid the threat to his identity by withdrawing from the group's activity in spite of the isolation that this entails. Being a member of the large group can be a frightening experience and the question must be asked: 'What is its value, and what can be learned through this experience?' Perhaps the answer is to do with organizations and leadership and the realization that leaders last only as long as they provide what the group needs, whatever that may be. It also highlights the fact that in society and organizational life, so many actions, policies, and beliefs are based on myths and assumptions which no one dare question for fear of the answer that might be given. In a large group, it takes great courage for the still small voice to speak out against an action of which it disapproves and risk the hostility of the group. Finally, the realization comes that the 'goodness' or 'badness' of the group depends entirely on the 'goodness' and 'badness' of the group members.

(c) *The intergroup event.* This event was originally designed by Bridger in the second conference held in 1959 and with some modifications has remained a feature of these conferences ever since (Higgin and Bridger 1965). The aim of the event is to study intergroup relations, including the problem of exercising authority on behalf of others. As a member (the author has attended two Leicester conferences) this event can be experienced as the most bewildering of the whole conference. It commences with the conference director outlining the task of the event, the role of the staff, and the rooms available. The large group is then left to work out how it will organize itself in order to carry out the task, but inevitably the same thing happens. Members rush out to occupy rooms and so groups are formed on an irrational and panic-stricken basis. The instant and irrational formation of groups seems to be an automatic and inevitable occurrence in such an exercise. In the first intergroup event in 1959 Higgin and Bridger reported that groups were formed almost instantly. Rice reported that in all the conferences he directed, members had left the room to form groups in less than a minute.

After such hasty and unplanned action, members inevitably start to analyse the basis on which their own group has formed and attempt to formulate their task. After a while, some members change (or attempt to change) groups, but one factor that always occurs is that of representation. Each group wants to know what the other groups are doing and this results in the appointment of representatives and 'plenipotentiaries' who attempt to communicate with other groups. Frequently a meeting is organized at which group representatives attend and attempt to formulate common plans and action on behalf of their groups, and these frequently result in disarray.

The role of the staff is to help the members learn and understand the nature of intergroup relations from the data emerging in the event. The staff group make their members available as consultants and will work with any groups providing they think the 'contract' they make will further the work of the event.

The event highlights the problem of the use and delegation of authority. Who speaks for whom and with what authority becomes the major question and this has particular relevance to interdepartmental communications in organizations and the problem of trade-union representation and negotiation.

The institutional event is similar to the intergroup event, but the emphasis is on the study of the relationships between the members and the staff group, who together make up the conference institution.

(*d*) *Application groups.* At the first conference in 1957 each application group was given a project outside the conference in an attempt to apply their learning to such organizations as schools and the police force. In all subsequent conferences, these external projects have been discontinued and the task of the application groups now is to relate the experience gained in the conference to the members' work in their sponsoring organizations. A recent innovation is orientation groups, which are similar to the application groups, but have, in addition, a meeting at the start of the conference that focuses on the implication of crossing the boundary into the conference and taking up a member role in it.

The author's experience is that, compared with the rest of the conference, these application groups are dull and lifeless; this may be for a variety of reasons. First, they are the only conference events dealing with the 'there and then' rather than the 'here and now'. Second, this activity arouses a great deal of anxiety concerning the value of the course and what has been gained from it. Each member has invested time and money in attending and all find it very difficult to conceptualize the precise nature of what has been learnt. A related problem is how will members communicate their experience to their bosses and colleagues. Finally, the application groups indicate that the conference is nearly over and highlights the sadness involved in ending the many and, frequently intense, relationships formed during the two weeks.

Evaluation of the Tavistock conferences

How effective are these conferences? There is no literature on the subject. Conferences continue to be held twice a year with a full membership indicating that they continue to meet a need in society. One interesting development is that the Tavistock model has been exported to America and an annual two week conference, sponsored by the Washington School of Psychiatry, is held at Mount Holyoke College, that is very close in philosophy and method to the Leicester conferences.

Other conferences have been organized in America, using the Tavistock model. Klein and Gould described one such conference, held at the Yale Summer High School, that was designed to help the development of disadvantaged adolescent boys (Klein and Gould 1973). Similar conferences have also been held in Canada.

*

Based on his own experiences, the author would attempt to make the following evaluation of the Tavistock/Leicester conferences.

Unique learning experience. It is a powerful experience. Members' emotions and feelings can become fully operative in what is for most people attending, a unique experience. To experience for oneself the fact that 'rational man' is driven and, at times, controlled by such powerful feelings as love and hate, and that these emotions contribute so much to organizational life, both in its structure and operation, is salutary, and provides the sort of learning that cannot be achieved through academic study.

Roles and role formation. The conference experience sharply reveals how roles are determined between the individual and the group (frequently by unconscious collusion) and are never simply assumed by the individual. Katz and Kahn have shown how organizational roles result from the individual complying with, or resisting, the influences 'sent' to him by people involved with his role (the role set) (Katz and Kahn 1966). In these conferences, a similar process is at work that determines the social roles played by members. This process is especially obvious in the large group where, for instance, a person who tells a joke can rapidly become the 'court jester' through the members projecting that role on to him. At the same time, this implies that other roles are withheld and so the person can be locked in a straight-jacket and made the buffoon of the group. A similar process can happen with someone who is angry. He can easily be given the role of 'angry man' by the group, and through projective identification be made to carry the group's anger. This role can rapidly develop into that of 'scape-goat', with the belief that all the group's problems and difficulties stem solely from that person and would disappear if only he would leave. Resulting from these experiences a person becomes aware of the processes that result in both organizational and social roles and hence he should have more ability to influence the role he wishes to take, whether in work or in a social setting and so prevent the deskilling that can easily occur.

Authority and the staff role. One of the strange things to realize after such a conference is that there are no rules constraining members' behaviour. At any time members are free to do what they want (including leaving) but the power of the group, whether large or small, is at all times constraining and influencing individual behaviour, just as much as a written list of rules. Sometimes, behaviour occurs which is more extreme than 'normal', but it is usually carried out in a rather self-conscious manner. For instance at one conference a group formed in the institutional event which called itself 'the delinquents' and proceeded to behave in a manner suitable to that title. At one stage, it 'kidnapped' a member of staff, but in truly British fashion, released him when it was time for tea!

*

Central to the authority exercised in the conference is the role of the staff. At the start of the conference, the staff are the only members of the institution who have a clear idea of a conference role. However, it is a 'detached' role that concentrates on the transference relationship between the group and the staff member, who is always perceived by the group as an authority figure. By remaining in this role throughout the sessions and, for instance, by entering and leaving groups precisely on time, the staff set a sharp boundary between themselves and the groups. In these situations, feelings and phantasies about authority figures are projected on to the staff, who attempt to help members check phantasy against reality and thus enable them to modify their behaviour towards authority. Because of this, the words, and even the looks, of the staff can be experienced by members as reprimands, and suggestions heard as commands. Referring to this phenomena, Turquet wrote:

'An interpretation from a consultant is often treated as a

rebuke: "We have got it wrong again". It may also be treated as a specific instruction to do something. Thus when a whole conference membership of fifty or so assembled to study inter-group relations, heard the statement "It seems that in order to carry out this exercise some process of small group formation will have to be thought about", it was taken as an instruction to divide, and the room cleared itself in a matter of seconds.'

(Turquet 1974: 361)

At the same time, this places enormous power in the hands of the staff, who are aware of these processes and therefore must be continually aware of the influence they can exert. It is for this reason that most staff members are psychoanalysts or clinical psychologists or have attended at least two such conferences as members with some further training.

On the final evening, the staff come out of their role and meet the members at an informal social gathering. Although this is not part of the official timetable it provides one of the most significant events for members, allowing them to discover that their consultant, until then possibly phantasized as a stoney-hearted, intransigent ogre, is in fact a normal human being.

The implications for organizational life are obvious. Members realize that the 'boss' in any setting will be the focal point for the phantasies of his subordinates concerning authority figures and that these phantasies will be projected on to him. This should encourage members to test out their own feelings and relationships with their superiors and see how much is reality and how much is their own projection. Correspondingly, this helps members to realize the power they have in authority positions and to consider how they use it.

Influence on society

The original 1957 conference was largely due to requests for training and development from industry and at that conference almost 50 per cent of the members came from industry and commerce. However, since then the composition of the membership has changed and *Table 2* (see over) gives an analysis of the membership of three conferences.

Table 2   *Membership of Tavistock conferences (%)*

Sponsoring organizations	1957	1972	1976
Industry/commerce	45	20	26
Universities/colleges/schools	18	25	20
Social services	18	11	–
Prison/probation	14	9	10
Members of Tavistock	–	11	11
Psychiatrists and psychiatric social workers	–	21	32
Others	5	3	1

These figures reveal a definite trend in membership away from industry and commerce and a move towards clinical and related work with a significant part of the membership coming from the Tavistock Institute and Clinic. Whether such trends are seen as good or bad must remain a value judgement. One of the reasons for the change in membership is due to other conferences being organized on a similar model but for specific organizations. The Grubb Institute (formerly called Christian Teamwork Institute) runs courses and conferences mainly directed towards similar organizations. The University of Bristol's Department of Education, the Treasury Department, Tube Investments, and Unilever are among some of the British organizations that have either asked the Tavistock staff to run conferences for them or have developed their own in consultation with them.

In the American conferences the membership has reflected the fact that the sponsoring institutions were identified with psychiatry and in the first conference 76 per cent of the members came from the field of mental health. In the 1968 conference the figure had changed to 61 per cent and those responsible considered this to be a desirable trend. However, in the author's own judgement, the main cause for the trend in the British conferences towards a clinical membership and away from industrial management lies in the conference model itself. There is no doubt that this form of training creates, or reveals, a great deal of hostility. The conference does not generate much happiness, nor is it meant to. However, it does generate hostile and angry feelings in many of the events that are unpleasant to experience, either personally or vicariously. It can be argued that such feelings are indissoluble components of all human relations and unless they are revealed and confronted, there is little likelihood of learning and improvement in this field. Rice wrote:

'Because relations between leaders and followers must be based on their mutual dependence, the stresses and conflicts caused by these antithetic feelings have to be dealt with, suppressed or otherwise controlled whenever decisions have to be taken. Any understanding of the problems of leadership must therefore take account of the potential destructiveness of the hostility inherent in all interpersonal and intergroup relations.'
(Rice 1965: 175)

Such intense hostile feelings are very difficult for the ordinary non-clinically experienced manager to deal with, and many have difficulty in seeing the relevance to their own work roles. On the other hand, clinically trained members, though not immune to these feelings, are more likely to be working in overt emotional situations in their normal work. Thus for them, the conference works in areas with which they are more familiar and which is closer to their work experience. Consequently, they are more likely to relate their experience to their own work roles.

Another aspect of the conference which may affect membership composition concerns the staff role. Members can, at times, feel strongly that the staff are critical, remote, and very authoritarian. The model explains this in terms of projection and therefore any criticism or opposition from members to the staff is interpreted in these terms. Nevertheless, these feelings are real and if they are not worked through may remain in the memory of the members, so that the staff, when they are remembered, continue to be thought of as critical authoritarians.

Clinically oriented members, especially those with analytic experience, may be better equipped to understand these processes and realize the dynamics of this behaviour. Managers, on the other hand, are less likely to have these theoretical models, and may well remain confused after the event. Clearly, if the memory of these events is completely unpleasant, then organizations are unlikely to sponsor further members.

8 Human behaviour and general systems theory

A phenomenon of the twentieth century has been the increasing association and integration of academic disciplines and sciences that previously were considered to be separated by rigid boundaries. The progress made in the study of some of the basic units of life, such as the complex molecules of haemoglobin and DNA, is due to the co-operation of workers in the field of organic chemistry, biology, and crystallography. The current work in astronomy regarding quasars and 'black holes' reveals the close links between astronomers dealing with stars of enormous size and atomic physicists studying 'quarks' and other sub-atomic particles. This increasing co-operation and interconnection between the sciences is revealed in the general names by which groups of them are now referred to, such as the 'material' sciences (in organic chemistry, physics, crystallography, and so forth) and the 'life' sciences (medicine, biology, and so forth).

This process of integration has also occurred in those disciplines dealing with the study of human behaviour. The 'behavioural' sciences include theories and evidence taken mainly from psychology, sociology, and anthropology. Each of these fields of study looks at human behaviour from a particular perspective, but they can combine to make significant new contributions to the understanding of man in his world.

Psychoanalysis, although primarily concerned with understanding human behaviour in terms of the individual psyche at the intra-personal level, has always been concerned with human relations in groups and organizations. Such seminal thinkers as Freud and Ferenczi sought to understand the processes by which individuals formed groups and their behaviour within them. Bion demonstrated that the difference between an effective and ineffective group lay in the former being in touch with reality, while the latter is cut off from it being concerned only with its internal emotions and phantasies.

Consequently, any other approach to behaviour that is concerned with the relationship of a group to its external environment should be ideally suited to complement psychoanalytic theory. This chapter will show that 'general systems theory' has provided just such ideas and concepts and that these have become integrated in order to give new insights into the behaviour and operation of groups and organizations.

General systems theory

The *Shorter Oxford Dictionary* defines a system as 'a whole composed of parts in orderly arrangement according to some scheme or plan. A set or assemblage of things connected, associated, or interdependent, so as to form a complex unity'. The word was used in 1779 to describe the universe and in the nineteenth century it was used to describe the planetary and solar systems, a system of telegraph wires, and the low pressure system associated with a cyclone. However, it was not until the early part of the twentieth century that systems were studied as a discrete concept and, especially under the influence of von Bertalanffy, a 'general systems theory' emerged. This theory attempts to describe the nature of systems in general and has made a considerable impact on most aspects of thought, from psychiatry to computer science.

Originally classical physics developed well-defined laws concerning inanimate systems, which involved chemical and physical reactions. These precise laws deal with energy transfers and are stated in the laws of thermo-dynamics. The second law of thermo-dynamics says basically that the energy of every system is decreasing until it finally reaches a steady state of maximum homogeneity when, by definition, no work can be done by the system. A simple example of this is an electric battery, which is a system of lead plates and acid. When the reaction between the lead and acid is completed the battery goes 'flat' because the system has reached a steady state and no further work, in the form of electric current, can be obtained from it.

Yet these laws of physics do not apply to systems that involve life processes. Von Bertalanffy, who was one of the major thinkers in this area, put the contradiction in this way:

> 'According to the second law of thermo-dynamics, the general trend of events in physical nature is towards states of maximum disorder and levelling down of differences, with the so-called heat death of the universe as the final outlook, when all energy is degraded into evenly distributed heat of low temperature, and the world process comes to a stop. In contrast, the living world shows, in embryonic development and in evolution, a transition towards higher order, heterogeneity and organization.'   (von Bertalanffy 1968: 40)

This dichotomy can be expressed as the difference between the views and theories of Lord Kelvin and Charles Darwin, the former expressing the law of degradation in physics and the latter the law of evolution in biology. Kelvin's theories are in opposition to Darwin's, although both can be said to describe systems. In a seminal essay, von Bertalanffy solved the problem by using the concepts of 'closed' and 'open' systems (von Bertalanffy 1969). A 'closed' system is one that is independent of its environment and where a steady state is achieved through chemical equilibria, which is describable by the laws of thermo-dynamics. When the system reaches this final steady state no further work can be obtained from it. The previous example of an electric battery is therefore an illustration of a 'closed' system.

In contrast to this, the 'open' system is continually in contact with its environment, importing energy, converting, and then exporting the transformed energy back to the environment. This is of the greatest importance to all living systems because, as von Bertalanffy wrote: 'In biology, the nature of the open system is at the basis of fundamental life phenomena' (von Bertalanffy 1969: 83). The human cell provides a good illustration of a biological open system. While the cell appears to remain constant, it is in fact continually renewing itself by importing appropriate chemicals from its environment, that is, the bloodstream. These change processes are so precisely controlled that the cell maintains a steady state. However, the steady state achieved by the living cell is clearly of a different nature from the steady state of the flat battery. There is continual change and adaptation taking place in the former and, unlike the closed system, work is being done by the cell. The cell's effectiveness (that is, the healthy cell) is determined by the maintenance of a balance between itself and the environment (that is, the bloodstream) and if this balance fails the cell will malform or die.

This example also illustrates the importance of the boundary in an open system, for it becomes obvious that it is the exchanges at the boundary, both import and export, that enable an open system to maintain its dynamic equilibrium.

A significant difference between open and closed systems is that open systems can reach the same final state from different initial conditions. This phenomenon, called 'equifinality', is illustrated in biology, where a half-germ of a sea-urchin will develop into a complete sea-urchin, which is inexplicable in physiochemical terms. In human terms the same principle is revealed in a child who, through sickness, is severely underdeveloped, but later recovers and achieves normal growth. The importance of this concept for organizations will be shown later, when it emerges in terms of organizational choice.

General systems theory and the individual

Although the concept of open systems was developed in the field of biology it can be applied to people and organizations. One of the most interesting applications was made by Rice, who wrote: 'An individual may be seen as an open system. He exists and can exist only through processes of exchange with his environment' (Rice 1969: 574).

The system in this case consists of the internal world of the individual, comprising his beliefs and expectations together with his primitive inborn impulses and the controls that he has developed over them. Nevertheless, he exists as an open system and must interact with the world in which he lives, continually striving to maintain a balance between his own internal needs and the demands of others. Rice said that this function is carried out by the ego: 'The mature ego is one that can define the boundary between what is inside and what is outside and can control the transactions between the one and the other' (Rice 1969: 574).

However, the individual is not a single but a multi-task system, and problems of control arise when a specific task has to be done that does not require all the available activities of which the individual is capable. To perform a specific task, an individual must take on a specific role, and each role or task system has to be composed of relevant skills, experience, feelings, and attitudes. Rice illustrates these ideas in the following diagram:

Figure 8   The role system of the individual

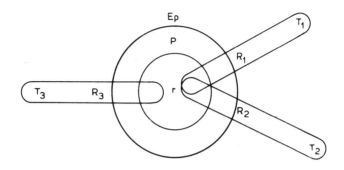

Ep	=	External environment of individual
P	=	Ego-function
r	=	Internal world of individual
T_1 etc	=	Tasks
R_1 etc	=	Roles

Source: Rice (1969: 575)

This diagram shows how a person undertakes different roles in order to perform different tasks. For instance, a person may be called on during a day to perform three very different tasks, each of which requires a different combination of personal skills and attitudes. The first task (T^1) may be to supervise a subordinate at work, the second (T^2) to give a lecture, and the third (T^3) may be to play with his children when he returns home. Each task requires the individual to mobilize the appropriate skills, feelings, and attributes from his total mental resources (and to suppress those that are not needed) and so play the different roles of manager (R^1), teacher (R^2), and father (R^3). The success of each role in terms of effectiveness will depend on the balance and integration maintained between the needs and resources of the individual and the requirements of the external world, that is, the demands made by the subordinate, the lecture audience, and his children respectively. Because different roles require different skills, the ego must require different skills, the ego must exercise a management control function that consists of three elements.

(i) The mobilization of skills and emotions appropriate for the role performance.

(ii) The control of transactions with the environment, so that the inputs and outputs (that is, behaviour) are appropriate.

(iii) The control and suppression of other activities that are within the total resources of the individual but that are irrelevant to the particular task.

The organization as an open system

So far, general systems theory, and the concept of 'open' systems, has been used to illuminate the processes at work in biology and in the individual human being. However, the same approach can be used to analyse and describe the processes at work in an organization.

An organization, such as a manufacturing company, is a complex system of interrelated departments, processes, and people. There is clearly a boundary between what is 'inside' the organization and what is 'outside', although different people may locate this boundary at different positions. The organization is an open system in that it exists within an environment and must continually import energy, materials, and people from that environment. These imports are used within the system to create whatever goods or services are being produced, and then exported back into the environment with an added value. As with all open systems the organization maintains a steady state only as long as it continually changes and adapts to the forces outside. In business terms, the organization develops and maintains its effectiveness as long as it reacts to the changing needs of the market and of society in general by responding to them with the appropriate products. *Figure 9* (see over) illustrates a manufacturing company as an open system.

However, the systems approach also reveals the essential nature of management. Open systems depend on the appropriate exchanges taking place between what is inside and what is outside. It is these essential processes that maintain the dynamic equilibrium

Figure 9   A manufacturing company viewed as an open system

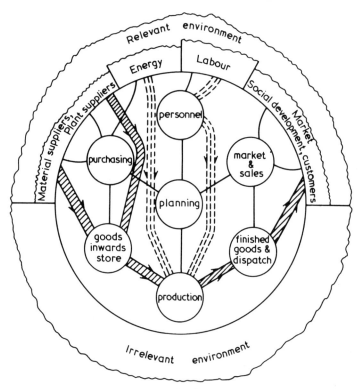

and the ongoing life of the system. In the healthy biological cell, these processes are automatic and are part of the life-process. In the individual, the ego performs these functions and this is the key to the maintenance of mental health and effective behaviour. However, in the organization, these boundary exchanges are the essential responsibility of management. The organization is effective in as far as management is aware of the reality outside the organization, which will involve customers, suppliers, financial availability, the labour market, social trends, and government legislation.

Management must then react and proact (initiating action) to these realities by ensuring that their organization can meet these demands in terms of appropriate organizational structure and behaviour, and produce a product that meets the market needs.

Management can now be seen to be essentially boundary management, and delegation not simply a choice but a necessity. Within an organization, each department can be seen as a sub-system, with the difference that the boundary of each sub-system will frequently adjoin other sub-systems, and the environment will, in that case, consist only of internal organizational life. For instance in the diagram, the planning department when seen as a sub-system, has a boundary which interfaces with personnel, market and sales, production, and purchasing. In this instance (although this is unlikely to happen in real life) the environment of the planning department consists entirely of other internal parts within the organization. Yet the personnel department, for instance, is shown to have a boundary that interfaces with an environment that consists of parts outside the organization, that is, the labour market, and also within, that is, the planning department.

The concept of 'equifinality' also illuminates organizations when they are considered as open systems. In a closed system, the final steady state is inevitable and the initial situation directly determines the end result. Yet open systems, because they are constantly changing and renewing, can achieve the same steady state from different starting points. For organizations, this implies choice. The organization, through the management function, can choose the way in which it will react to external forces from a variety of market strategies and by a variety of internal structures and procedures. The systems approach to organizations reveals that organizational change is not a rare occurrence that must be avoided as long as possible, but an essential part of a continuous process through which the organization maintains its effectiveness. One of the major problems facing all organizations today is how to react appropriately to an environment where change is so rapid that it produces turbulence.

Trist and Bamforth and 'socio-technical systems'

The concept of open systems theory was first applied to an actual organization by Trist and Bamforth and the results published in 1951. Following the nationalization of the British coal-mining industry in 1948, mechanical methods were increasingly introduced into the mines and these had a considerable effect on both the behaviour of the miners and the productivity of the mines. The major change involved the use of mechanical coal-cutters, which needed to work at long lengths of the coal-seam resulting in the 'longwall' method of mining. Trist and Bamforth spent over two years in close discussion with face-workers and mine-managers in an attempt to discover the effect of this changing technology on the social structure, which they described as a 'psycho-social whole'. Their initial statement shows the centrality of the systems concept to their research: 'In the account to follow, the longwall method will be regarded as a technological system expressive of the prevailing outlook of mass-production engineering and as a social structure consisting of the occupational roles that have been institutionalised in its use' (Trist and Bamforth 1951: 5).

Before the introduction of mechanical methods the basic working unit was a pair of miners with one or two assistants, who were all self-chosen and who made their own contract with management regarding the amount of coal to be hewn and the wages to be paid. Each pair was multi-skilled and multi-tasked, and responsible for the entire cycle of operations. Leadership and supervision were internal to the group and they could set their own targets and stop at whatever point they wished. There were no organization structures between these small groups and the total colliery, and so an interrelated system developed that maintained the social balance. Trist and Bamforth described this situation as one where each small group exhibits 'responsible autonomy'.

With the introduction of mechanization, mainly in the form of conveyer belts and coal-cutters, the working of a single coal face 180-200 yards long became possible. However, these technological changes inevitably caused changes in the way individuals were organized and also affected their working and personal relationships.

A new structure emerged to cope with the 'longwall' method, which consisted of a shift-cycle group of forty to fifty men together with shot-firers and deputies. This generated the basic conflict, for the new technology gave rise to social and psychological problems that were new to the miners and contrary to their traditions. The longwall method had a three-shift cycle with each shift responsible for a specific task in the cycle, namely cutting, ripping, and filling. This resulted in what Trist and Bamforth called a 'spatio-temporal structure' where forty men were spread out over 200 yards over a twenty-four hour period. This was a very different situation from the original 'single-place' working, where two men worked on a ten-yard face.

Within the total cycle there were seven different roles, and a face-worker was trained in only one of these and was unlikely to change roles. Again, this was completely different from the single-place working, where each miner had been a complete collier who needed to have all the skills necessary to carry out a variety of tasks. Most significantly, the three shifts never met, so that the conditions for 'responsible autonomy' were absent. Little if any social integration could be achieved between workers either on the same shift, or between different shifts.

This problem was illustrated by what happened on the third shift, whose specific job was to load the coal on to the conveyers. On this shift twenty individuals each worked on a ten-yard 'stint' but there was little contact between them and none with the cutters who had cut the coal on the previous shift and on whom they were completely dependent. The situation was one where twenty men of unequal skills and abilities faced equal lengths of coal face with unequal conditions. 'There is little doubt that these circumstances contribute to the widespread incidence of psycho-somatic and kindred neurotic disorders among those concerned' (Trist and Bamforth 1951: 30).

As a result certain kinds of behaviour arose among the fillers which, the writers said, were defences against these anxieties and hindered the overall effectiveness of the primary task — to get coal. Some informal groups arose among the fillers who agreed to help each other. Inevitably these did not include the 'bad' and the weak workers, who were left with an even more insecure role than before. There was strong competition for the best work places and this prevented the development of any team spirit. If a crisis occurred, the fillers blamed the previous shifts and vice versa and no one would take responsibility. In fact, this scapegoating was an example of projective identification whereby one shift projected its anxieties on to another and then attacked them. In Bion's terms, this showed that the shift, as a group, was working on the basic assumption of fight/flight and its energy was mobilized in fight/flight behaviour rather than in achieving an effective output in the work group.

The conclusions of this study were simple and precise. 'A qualitative change will have to be effected in the general character of the method [the longwall system], so that a social as well as a technological whole can come into existence' (Trist and Bamforth 1951: 37).

The 'socio-technical systems' approach

Trist's and Bamforth's work has made a considerable impact on the field of organization and management and has given rise to a number of further studies, which will be discussed later. Their detailed analysis is based on system concepts and records how these ideas can illuminate behaviour in organizations. However, their special contribution lies in their analysis of the interrelation between the technological and the social structures in an organization and how each influences the other. From this the concept of 'socio-technical systems' was developed. (In fact this term is never used by Trist and Bamforth in their paper. Although all the concepts associated with this term are clearly expressed, it appears that the actual term was not used by Trist until 1953).

The major components within an organizational system are the technological aspects concerning the machinery, the particular method of working, and the social aspects that involve the interpersonal relation between the employees. These components are interlinked with each other and changes in one will automatically cause changes in the other. The whole system can now be perceived as a 'socio-technical' system and its total effectiveness will depend on the balance achieved between the social and the technological components. This concept has particular importance for the management of change and innovation. Changes frequently involve new technology and processes, and the natural assumption is that these must be used to their maximum efficiency in order to produce the greatest increases possible. However, the concept of a 'socio-technical' system implies that the optimum level of technological usage is one that maintains a balance between technology and the people working in the system. It may happen that a new machine or process has to work below its optimum capacity in order to maintain its balance with the social structure of the organization.

Trist and Emery reviewed these findings almost ten years later and placed them firmly within the model of an open socio-technical system for the following reasons (Emery and Trist 1969). First, enterprises can definitely be considered as open systems because they have the following characteristics:

(i) they grow by processes of internal elaboration:
(ii) they manage to achieve a steady state while doing work: although there is a continuous throughput, the enterprise as a whole remains constant. This is described as a 'quasi-stationary equilibrium'.

To achieve this steady state, there must be regular commerce between the enterprise and other groups in the external social environment. Management is required at the boundary to allow for this commerce to be regularized, both within and outside the system. Within the enterprise, there must be an appropriate organization for men and materials. Equally, the system must be able to respond, both reactively and proactively, to external market forces.

However, the technical component within the enterprise plays a major role in 'import-conversion-export' processes, which is the essential process in the enterprise establishing a steady state. Hence, 'it follows that the open system concept must be referred to the socio-technical system, not simply to the social system of an enterprise' (Emery and Trist 1969: 284). This statement ties in precisely with Trist's and Bamforth's observations in the mines when they said:

'So close is the relationship between the various aspects that the social and psychological can be understood only in terms of the detailed engineering facts and of the way the technological system as a whole behaves in the environment of the underground situation.'   (Trist and Bamforth 1951: 11)

The Ahmedabad experiment

A further example of the way in which general systems theory has been used to analyse and improve organizational structure and behaviour is provided by the work carried out by Rice in the mid-fifties in India (Rice 1958). Rice was approached by the chairman of a textile mill in Ahmedabad where management and workers were experiencing many problems owing to the introduction of automatic weaving looms.

Unlike the coal-mining studies, where Trist and Bamforth took the role of scientific observers, Rice was in the role of 'action researcher' where he not only collected research material, but also acted as consultant to the company and helped to initiate change. Rice placed the work he did (referred to as the 'Ahmedabad experiment') in a systems context. In his book, which describes this work, he wrote:

> 'In the experiments, attempts were made to take into account both the independent and interdependent properties of the social, technological and economic dimensions of existing socio-technical systems, and to establish new systems in which all dimensions were more adequately interrelated than they had previously been.'   (Rice 1958: 4)

The concept of the primary task. Before describing the experiment, Rice set forth some of the concepts and assumptions underlying his work; one of the most interesting is the 'primary task'. This concept derives from Bion's theory, which states that when a group is operating as a work group, that is, working effectively and co-operatively and not influenced by basic assumptions, it is attempting to achieve a specific task. 'When a group meets, it meets for a specific task, and in most human activities today, co-operation has to be achieved by sophisticated means' (Bion 1968: 98). This primary task, in systems terms, is the task that each system or sub-system is created to perform. Rice saw it as the rallying point for effective co-operation from people in the system.

> 'The performance of the primary task is supported by powerful social and psychological forces which ensure that a considerable capacity for co-operation is evoked among the members of the organisation created to perform it. As a direct corollary, the effective performance of a primary task can provide an important source of satisfaction for those engaged upon it.'   (Rice 1958: 33)

Rice gave three other assumptions about task organization,

which although written twenty years ago, are relevant to current discussions on job enrichment.

(i) A task should be so organized that it is a 'whole' task.

(ii) Those engaged on the task should be able to control their own activities.

(iii) Tasks should be so organized that people can form satisfactory relationships.

The automatic looming shed. By 1953 the Jubilee Mills at Ahmedabad had, as a part of its total production system, one experimental shed containing 224 automatic looms. However, the introduction of these machines had failed to increase productivity, which remained the same as, or slightly less, than the output obtained from the non-automatic machines. The experimental shed was organized on a shift system, each shift consisting of twenty-nine workers who carried out twelve activity roles. Apart from a small group concerned with loom tuning and maintenance (the 'jobbers'), each man worked separately, forming not a group but merely an aggregate. This meant that the shift supervisor had twenty-seven individuals reporting to him, who were graded and paid on nine different scales. To add to this confusion of relationships two important control functions, inspection and production study, were carried out by departments external to the looming shed. *Figure 10* (see over) shows the organization of one shift of the automatic looming shed. This chart clearly demonstrates the complex network of relationships that existed owing to the shift-supervisor having to have a direct relationship with twenty-seven people.

This situation contradicted many of the assumptions and principles previously conceived of by Rice. There were no identifiable groups or sub-systems with clearly defined boundaries so that no worker could be committed to a primary task. Each of the twenty-seven workers had a separate and different task and so there could be no co-operation. There were no whole tasks, only activities, and these process activities controlled the worker and not vice versa. Finally, no satisfactory relationships could be formed among the workers themselves. Each person sought a special relationship with the supervisor, which encouraged a

Figure 10 Organization chart of one shift of the automatic loom shed

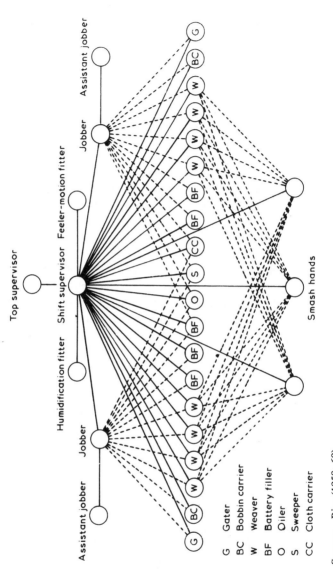

G   Gater
BC Bobbin carrier
W   Weaver
BF Battery filler
O   Oiler
S   Sweeper
CC Cloth carrier

Source: Rice (1958: 60)

similar pattern of 'reactive individualism' noted by Trist and Bamforth among the coal-miners.

Rice, in consultation with the management, attempted to develop a new organization that would not only utilize the productive capacity of the automatic looms but also enable an appropriate and supportive social structure to emerge. His basic idea was to create 'a group of workers for a group of looms'. It was worked out theoretically that a group of sixty-four looms could be managed by a group of seven workers, with one acting as a group leader. Another important change was to be the rationalization of the pay structure, with only three grades in place of the previous seven.

The plan was to hold proper discussions, experiment with one group, and monitor the results. Yet in some ways, the proposals were too successful. Within a day of putting forward the plan as a tentative proposal and 'through a complex process of mutual choice far too rapid to permit investigation' (Rice 1958: 70) the workers themselves organized two experimental groups on two shifts and management allowed those self-chosen groups to operate.

This first experimental period lasted for fifty-nine working days, and after thirty-seven days the remaining looms were reorganized on the same pattern. After the first few days, production figures rose and damage figures fell. Production which had previously been at a level of 80 per cent efficiency now rose to 95 per cent and damage fell from 30 per cent to an average of 20 per cent. Another similar reorganization was carried out with non-automatic looms, with similar significant increases in productivity.

Conclusions from the experiment. The results from the Ahmedabad experiment are very much in line with the coal-mining studies of Trist and Bamforth, but they add something extra to the ideas of supervision and management. They show that the man-task system is incomplete and requires management to control and co-ordinate the system at the boundary. Prior to the reorganization in the automatic loom shed, the supervisor was forced to intervene in the activities of the shed because every worker was directly controlled by him. After the reorganization only four group leaders reported to him, and this allowed him to carry out his proper task of boundary management, while allowing the workers to get on with their work. 'The significance of the difference between these two organisations rests ... in the emergence of clearly distinct areas of command which contain within themselves a relatively independent set of work roles with the skills necessary to govern their task boundaries' (Emery and Trist 1969: 292).

Another conclusion reached by Rice was that technology and technological progress need not be the main determinant of organizational social structures. For instance, the mass-production technology of the United States reflects the culture of a country whose future is not bounded by its past. Yet in India, the 'groups of workers for groups of looms' reflected much more the Indian system of small village communities, which has existed for centuries, and may have been one of the reasons why the new organization was taken up so enthusiastically by the workers. However, the Ahmedabad experiment showed 'that the assumption, often unconscious, that technology must completely determine social organization, need not go unchallenged' (Rice 1958: 253).

It also illustrates one of the concepts of general systems theory, namely 'equifinality'. An open system can achieve a steady state from a variety of initial situations and in different ways. This implies that an enterprise can exercise organizational choice and that a variety of structures can achieve a steady state, that is, operational effectiveness. Because of their interrelationships, the technological aspect of the system cannot be maximized in isolation. The social aspect must also be considered and a steady state will only be achieved when the technological and the social structures are harmonized into a socio-technical system. The corollary is that changes in one of these aspects will cause changes in the other, and this requires control and co-ordination by management if the steady state is to continue. This implies work at the boundary of the enterprise: 'If management is to control internal growth and development it must in the first instance control the "boundary conditions" — the forms of exchange between the enterprise and its environment' (Emery and Trist 1969: 294).

Rice continued to act as consultant to the company, until his death in 1969, and published a second book in 1963 that continued the story of management reorganization and gave up-dated information on the loom shed experiments.

In 1970, Miller, who had worked with Rice in Ahmedabad, visited the company and reviewed the socio-technical systems which Rice had introduced. While many changes had occurred during the seventeen years, the 'group' system survived almost completely, in spite of this period being one of considerable social and industrial change. Miller wrote:

'This suggests that the assumptions on which Rice worked have been largely substantiated. It also suggests that, quite independently of any notion of "industrial democracy", the goal of designing systems to minimise the chances of disaster may be more appropriate to industrial organisations than is generally recognised.'   (Miller 1975: 385)

Systems theory applied to the north-west Durham coalfield

Trist's and Bamforth's original survey in 1951 of the consequences of the longwall method of coal-mining had surveyed the British mining situation as a whole. Following on from this, Trist and a team of co-workers studied the mines in the north-west Durham coalfield between 1955 and 1958. They used the concept of an open, socio-technical system as their frame of reference. This work, published in 1963 as *Organizational Choice*, is important because (following an analysis of the situation) actual changes were proposed and implemented, and measurements were made of the resulting performance differences (Trist, Higgin, Murray, and Pollock 1963).

This work, like Rice's Indian experiment, concerned the introduction of new methods of production that had failed to produce the expected increases in output. Mining communities are traditionally close-knit and the social structures, both in the pit and outside it, have developed within the harsh environment of poverty, physical danger, and exploitation. The Durham area provided a good example of these traditions and any changes which caused a break with these were likely to cause resentment and hostility. In the mines, the traditional method of work organization was called the 'single place working' where pairs of miners worked on a small part of the coal face and between them carried out all the activities needed to get coal. This traditional method involved three elements that had developed over the years and that profoundly affected the miner's life at work. First, the men who worked the particular place on the coal face formed closely-knit, co-operative groups called 'marrow' groups (marrow refers to mate). These groups consisted of six men, that is, two men on three shifts, who worked the same place and who were self-selected and paid on a common pay-note. Second, the tradition of 'cavilling' had evolved as a unique feature in this area. Every quarter, all work places were pooled and drawn by lot ('cavilled') at a formal ceremony at which management and union officials were present. This method had evolved as a safeguard against favouritism and victimization. Thirdly, the men were paid on a contract system whereby the group negotiated a price for a certain amount of coal and then distributed this money among themselves. This method resulted in the group managing itself and consequently the mine managers had little need to use their formal authority. All these traditions contributed to a situation where the working group exercised a high degree of responsible autonomy.

The introduction of mechanization in the mines, and especially the use of coal-cutting machines, changed these traditional working arrangements, with the disruption of established human relationships. Because the coal-cutters could now work a 100 yard coal face, each shift performed only one operation. On the first shift, the coal was cut and then dislodged with explosives. The second shift loaded the coal onto the conveyers and set the roof supports. On the third shift, the conveyers were advanced and the gateways to the coal face enlarged.

This new method of working (the 'longwall' method) represented a sharp break with the tradition of single-place working. The old 'marrow-groups', where each man felt a close interdependence with his colleagues, were disbanded and the miners found themselves working on a shift with a large number of people they did not know, and in conditions that hindered the formation of relationships and team spirit.

Instead of being able to use all the varied skills that they had acquired, they now had work that required only one basic skill, which was carried out independently of their fellows.

There was also a significant change in the method of wage payment. Instead of the old contract method, a complex price system was devised, which was related to many different criteria, such as yardage, tonnage, number of operations, and so forth depending on the job. The wage system was no longer a source of management control and, therefore, executive managers had to carry this burden, managers who were usually outside the face group. Consequently, 'Officials feel that they get no support from the men to maintain the cycle. The feelings of disappointment, rejection and anger that this experience generates discolour relations' (Trist, Higgin, Murray, and Pollock 1963: 64).

Yet some of the old traditions remained although thoroughly inappropriate to the new situation. For instance, many of the mining jobs were still 'cavilled' every quarter, which meant that work teams were being continually broken up and reformed. This led to instability in the work group and limited the investment an individual worker would put into his work.

Introduction of the 'composite longwall method'. Up to this stage, the work of Trist *et al.* appears to be similar to the earlier work of Trist and Bamforth. However, in the Durham coalfield a new system evolved which enabled comparisons to be made between the different social structures and emphasized the possibility of organizational choice. Following a year of intensive negotiations between union and management an innovation in work organization was made on the Manley coal-seam called the 'composite longwall method'. A self-selected group of forty-one men formed a shift cycle and allocated tasks and shifts among themselves. Equally important, they were all paid on a common pay-note, with a wage composed of 58 per cent basic wage and 42 per cent output bonus.

This method re-established at least four characteristics of the traditional method of single-place working:

(i) There was task continuity — each on-coming shift took up the operation cycle at the point left by the previous shift.

(ii) Multi-skills and multi-tasks — the miners were able, and were also required, to use a variety of skills since they were faced with a variety of different tasks.

(iii) Work groups — the groups were self-selected like the marrow groups, with the result that interdependent relations could be formed both within each shift and throughout the three shifts.

(iv) Common payment — there was a common pay-note, which included a group bonus, and this placed the responsibility for all the work on the team as a whole.

Improved results. Comparative studies were made between the original longwall method and the 'composite' longwall method developed at the Manley coal seam and the results showed clearly that the latter method had definite advantages.

In terms of work output, the composite method gave a productivity figure of 95 per cent whereas the conventional method had resulted in a figure of 78 per cent. In the conventional method, 31 per cent of the shift cycles were at normal levels but 69 per cent were lagging at the end of the filling shift. For the composite method, 73 per cent of the shift cycles were at normal levels and only 5 per cent were lagging. Most significantly 22 per cent were in advance of the planned target.

In the conventional method, the average team worked on only one activity and interacted with only one other activity group. The new method gave the miners approximately four main activities to perform and brought them into contact with five other groups. The overall improvement in morale was revealed in a significant reduction in absenteeism, which fell from 20 per cent to 8 per cent.

The end result was that not only was more coal produced, but it also became common for some of the sub-groups, if they had finished their scheduled work before time, to carry on working on the next activity in order to help their colleagues on the next shift. Miners using the new technology were now organized in such a way that they no longer felt that they were working under the tyranny of machines. In other words, an open socio-technical system was in operation and working in a steady state.

Conclusion — work and the nature of man

This chapter has examined the theory of general systems and analysed some of the practical work that it has generated, especially in those areas where organizations and work groups have been perceived as open socio-technical systems. These theories and the empirical evidence emphasize, in particular, the essential nature of the management function and show that this must occur at the system's boundary. It has also shown that the system must be balanced internally so that the man/machinery system may require a sub-optimizing of the technological aspect in order for the total system to operate efficiently. However, the systems approach, especially as shown in Trist's coal-mining studies and Rice's work in India, highlights one problem that has never been solved successfully in the majority of organizations. This problem is how to create and maintain an effective organization in which work can be done effectively but where, at the same time, the worker can exhibit and develop his essential humanity. Since the early days of Taylor and the emergence of mass production methods in organizations, there has been a constant struggle between the effective use of the most advanced mechanized production methods and the formation of jobs that provide the opportunity for employees to work in ways that are compatible with 'normal' human behaviour. Economic pressures and social attitudes have, in the main, caused technology to become the dominant factor in work. The market demands for relatively cheap goods and the desire for relatively well-paid jobs have resulted in organizations in which many workers use only a fraction of their abilities and gain scarcely any satisfaction in relation to their basic human needs. It is probably no longer the case that people are tyrannized by harsh management, but such systems can tyrannize all who work in them, both workers and 'bosses' alike, although in different ways. The alienation of people from their work and the impoverishment of the quality of working life are issues which are rapidly becoming central to the economic well-being of most industrialized countries. Employment can no longer be seen as the simple process of selling one's labour for money. The employee, whether shop-floor worker or managing director, is a total person who brings to work not only his skills, but also his emotional needs and a complete range of feelings. Work and the work situation must take this into account and when it does, the individual is able to gain many psychological benefits that are quite distinct from any economic returns. Sofer described this well when he wrote:

'Work provides the person with opportunities to relate himself to society, to contribute to society and to maintain a view of himself as a productive member of society through an output of goods and services. (The converse of this is widely recognised in the phenomenon of alienation.) Having a work role enables a man to maintain status and self-respect. Work roles structure the passage of time — and help to ward off depressing or distressing thoughts and feelings. At the level of unconscious personal dynamics, work keeps one in touch with reality, provides one with a sense of mastery and freedom and serves as a sublimation for sexual and aggressive impulses.'   (Sofer 1972: 228)

The essential and ongoing debate concerning man and work depends on the assumptions that are made about the nature of man. Many of these arguments have been based on political or religious viewpoints with which one may, or may not, agree, but some recent work has attempted to build on theories that (the proponents believe) are firmly grounded on objective psychological truths concerning man's nature and behaviour. One example is the theory advanced by Maslow who said that man's behaviour arises from the way in which he continually strives to satisfy his needs (Maslow 1970). These needs are a function of human existence and operate within a hierarchy of urgency, which can be categorized into five groups:

1   Physiological needs
2   Safety needs
3   Social needs
4   Ego needs
5   Self-actualization

A person is constantly motivated to satisfy these needs and at any one time his behaviour is directed to one of these five levels. The lowest unsatisfied set of needs in this hierarchy is the determinant of behaviour at any one time, but once satisfied it ceases to motivate and the next higher set of needs comes into operation. In Maslow's model, the highest needs are those which concern creativity and result in self-fulfilment. When this theory is translated into organizational behaviour it shows that people are motivated to work because of the actual work they are given and the situation in which the work is carried out. If the work itself provides opportunities for the satisfaction of personal needs, then the individual is motivated to work. The man-task system provides personal satisfaction and therefore results in the production of goods and services needed by the organization.

Herzberg developed Maslow's ideas and together with empirical data developed a theory of human motivation, which he called the 'motivation-hygiene' theory (Herzberg, Mausner, and Snyderman 1959). Herzberg believed that man has two sets of needs, which he continually tries to satisfy:

(a) The need to avoid pain and discomfort, and
(b) The need to grow and develop psychologically.

Some factors in organizations satisfy one set of needs and other factors satisfy the other set. The need to avoid pain and discomfort is satisfied by such organizational factors as company policy, supervision, salary, interpersonal relations, and working conditions. Although these factors (called 'hygiene' factors) must receive constant attention in order to prevent dissatisfaction, they cannot result in any long-term feelings of satisfaction. By the nature of the needs they meet, that is, the avoidance of pain and discomfort, they do not motivate a person to work well. On the other hand, the need to grow and develop psychologically is satisfied by such factors as achievement, recognition, responsibility, advancement, and work itself. These 'motivators' result in positive long-term feelings of satisfaction; therefore, if the worker can experience these factors in his work he is motivated to work.

This theory has been translated into practical terms in many organizations and is known as 'job enrichment'. A job is 'enriched' when the number and extent of Herzberg's 'motivators' are maximized. This has usually involved the restructuring of work so that the worker or work group has a greater variety of work to perform and a greater control and responsibility over the work process. In retrospect, the work of Trist and Rice can be seen as an approach to job enrichment and many of Rice's assumptions about the organization of tasks and roles are paralleled in this approach.

Maslow's and Herzberg's work is based on their particular view of the nature of man and both reflect a humanistic philosophy. Yet how far the concept of 'self-actualization' is a reflection of a particular American view of man and society and how far it describes a general behavioural truth is an open question. Nevertheless, their theories have helped to emphasize the important truth that organizations should be made for man and not vice versa, and underline Rice's statement that 'the assumption, often unconscious, that technology must completely determine social organisation need not go unchallenged' (Rice 1958: 253).

Jaques has taken a different approach in defining the nature of man and formulating a structure of organization that complements this. Jaques is both a Kleinian psychoanalyst and a specialist in organization and has combined analytic insights with practical knowledge of working organizations. In his book *A General Theory of Bureaucracy*, he wrote: 'the design of institutions must take into account and satisfy the nature of man and not be limited to satisfying the non-human criterion of technical efficiency of output' (Jaques 1976: 6). Jaques approached a definition of human nature by attempting to describe 'normal' behaviour. According to Jaques, as the human race has developed, certain characteristics of behaviour have emerged which are considered to enhance the value and survival of both self and society. Central to this idea is the notion that 'normal' behaviour involves and reinforces interaction between people. Therefore the characteristics of the 'normal' can include (at least):

(a) an awareness of self and the self of others
(b) the ability to communicate and understand the communication of others.
(c) the capacity to co-operate with another in paying attention to the same subject.
(d) the capacity for social and economic exchange relationships.

Having defined the normal man, it becomes clear that an appropriate and effective organization is one that enables man to function in such a normal way. Man's nature requires this, and therefore Jaques described such an organization as 'requisite'.

Requisite organizations facilitate the formation of relationships based on mutual trust and confidence. They are essentially open systems where work is done and where there are interchanges between the organization and its environment. On the other hand, anti-requisite organizations hinder and prevent the formation of normal relationships and are in fact 'paranoiagenic', that is, they create envy, hostile rivalry, and anxiety. They are closed systems preventing the interaction between man and his physical and social environment, with the result that social life runs down.

> 'The growth of human societies as open systems upon which the survival of the human species depends, requires a sufficient number of individuals who are free enough from persecutary anxiety to be able to take part in requisite social relationships, given the opportunity and the social setting necessary to do so: society already tends to call such individuals normal.'   (Jaques 1976: 8)

This statement by Jaques emphasizes the fact that the effectiveness of an organization depends on the extent to which 'normal' human behaviour is encouraged through the structure and methods used within it. The 'openness' of the system and the essential interchanges between the organization and its environment are a function of its individual members. This is in line with Bion's theory and shows that, in the last analysis, organizational behaviour is not only the sum of individual behaviour, but consists of the intra-personal behaviour of each member within the organization.

9 Organization as a defence against anxiety

It is ironic that as civilization develops and the major killing diseases of the past are gradually eradicated, there is a steady rise in modern stress diseases such as coronaries, hypertension, and mental ill-health. It is salutary to realize that in Britain with an adult population of 46 million, no less than 10 million people receive prescriptions for some kind of mind-affecting drug. While people grumble about losing 15 to 20 million working days a year through industrial disputes, something like 33 million working days a year are lost through ill-health.

Stress

The purpose in giving these facts is not to be alarmist, but rather to give the problem of stress its proper emphasis. First, stress is a real problem — a problem that causes at the personal level real pain and suffering. Second, at the organization level it causes disruption and loss of production.

Stress can only be fully understood if we go back to the very beginning of man's evolution. In their book, *The Imperial Animal* (1972) the authors (Tiger and Fox) emphasize that much of man's automatic behaviour, that is, our reactions and instincts, was developed and 'imprinted' on the species hundreds of thousands of years ago, when man was a hunter. They wrote: 'If we made an hour-long film to represent the history of tool-making man, industrial man would flash by in a few seconds at the end — he would barely be seen' (Tiger and Fox 1972: 21).

This means that man living in the complex electronic age of the twentieth century, has the automatic bodily reactions that evolved in a totally different culture and environment. The same authors wrote, 'We are wired for hunting — for the emotions, the excitements, the curiosities, the fears'.

So it is interesting to analyse what happened when primitive man found himself in imminent danger when he was out hunting. The two alternatives open to him were flight or fight, and therefore, through evolution, the body has developed automatic responses that assist in both these courses of action. First, the arteries near the skin clamped down, muscles tensed, and the blood pressure went up in relation to the heart beat increase, so that the body was ready for immediate action. Blood was forced out of the abdominal pool into the arms and legs where it was most needed to assist the muscles. The bowels emptied so that there was no unnecessary weight carried. Simultaneously, adrenalin was pumped into the blood-stream in order to help the blood clot quickly in case of wounding and consequent bleeding. As a result of all these internal physiological changes, man the hunter was more likely to get out of trouble fast, either by running like the wind or fighting furiously. When the danger was past the body resumed a less agitated functioning.

Immediately this gives a clue to the problem of stress in modern society. Stress is a condition in which the body reacts to danger in the same way as our hunting ancestors, *but spread over a long period*. The internal bodily changes, which were meant to last only a short time and were beneficial, may, in the stress situation, last for weeks or months and cause physical pain and damage to the body. Consequently, blood pressure may rise permanently and muscles remain tense with resulting pain and headaches. Digestion and the bowels may be affected, and if adrenalin is frequently going into the blood-stream, there will be a danger of clotting.

When man the hunter had fled from a bear or fought for his life, he slept in order to recover from the effects of his body's internal action. In a stress situation today, people are likely to feel continually tired, because they are never able to fully recover from the effects of their own bodies' internal activity. Paradoxically, the benefits of a good night's sleep may elude them owing to the brain's furious activity in trying to deal with its problems.

Finally, the other general symptom of stress manifests itself in an inability to concentrate on long-term plans or objectives. In the danger situation, the present is all that matters, the senses are stimulated to deal only with things that are immediate. People tend to behave without considering the long-term effects of their action. However, if the stress remains unresolved, tomorrow becomes yet another battle-field for self-preservation.

Stress can now be seen to result from a situation where a person feels threatened by danger and where his body automatically reacts in the same way man has always reacted, so as to preserve his life and safety. Yet the dangers faced by modern man have become much more complex and intangible, and far more difficult to deal with than that of a wild animal or an attacking savage. Those sorts of situations could be dealt with quickly, but for modern man, especially managers, locked into big organizations and carrying burdens of immense responsibility, the danger situation can last for a very long time with no easy solution.

Anxiety

There is no doubt that anxiety is central to all psychoanalytic theory and is probably the most important unpleasant feeling that human beings experience. Feelings of pleasure or of pain are highly subjective and it is extremely difficult to share them with another person. However, anxiety produces similar physiological effects on everyone. Everyone has experienced the pounding of the heart, sweating palms, rapid breathing and all the bodily tensions that anxiety automatically produces in the human body. The reason for these bodily changes are not hard to seek. Anxiety has always been a response to perceived danger. Through thousands of years of evolution man has developed two major responses to external danger — fight or flight. If primitive man was faced by a wild animal or a threatening stranger he either had to run away and avoid the danger or else stay and fight in order to overcome the threat. Only those who were successful in either of these strategies survived and gradually they became programmed into the human system becoming automatic responses to danger.

The physical effects of anxiety evolved originally as aids to survival, triggered off by dangerous situations. But while these physiological effects are commonly experienced by everyone, the causes of anxiety are intensely subjective and depend on the way in which each individual perceives and interprets the situation. In itself anxiety can lead to productive change and personal development. For instance, a manager at work may feel very anxious about a certain project he has to complete, but given the appropriate skills and resources, both human and technical, he will complete the project and in doing so, increase his ability to contain and master his anxiety. However, a different person in the same situation may experience such intense anxiety that he is unable to complete the task.

The opening paragraphs of this chapter showed that the effects of long-term unresolved anxiety result in the various bodily symptoms that are indicative of acute stress.

Neurotic anxiety

So far, anxiety has been considered as those feelings which are caused by an external source of danger and result automatically in physical bodily reactions. However, what of internal dangers, those subjective, frequently unconscious feelings and memories that can cause intense feelings of anxiety in a person, but which arise entirely from within the psyche?

The anxiety that arises from within the self is called 'neurotic' anxiety as opposed to 'objective' anxiety. Although they have different sources they are all experienced as the same painful emotional state.

The ego defences.   The normal actions that a person takes to deal with, or avoid, external anxiety are not appropriate to deal with internal neurotic anxiety. Consequently the ego develops additional ways to protect itself from these internal threats, which are called the 'ego defences'. They are usually agreed to be (a) repression, (b) regression, (c) sublimation, and (d) projection.

While they are all important aspects of behaviour, the ego defence of projection is the most important for the purpose of this chapter. Already one specific technique of projection has been explained (in the chapter on Melanie Klein) namely projective identification. However, simple projection occurs when a person unconsciously attributes to another person a characteristic that is in fact his own. Personal feelings of dislike, hatred, or envy that one person feels towards another and which give rise to internal feelings of neurotic anxiety are projected on to that person. The result is that instead of feeling 'I hate you' this is now experienced through projection as 'you hate me'. What was originally an internal threat is now experienced as an external threat and can be dealt with in the same way as all external threats, that is, by fight or flight. In fact the source of the anxiety remains within the self and there is only an apparent resolution of the anxiety. Until that is dealt with, it will keep manifesting itself as an external threat as in the extreme case of the paranoid who feels continually threatened by everyone with whom he comes in contact. The real source of the anxiety continues to remain within himself, and his continual conflict with people, although costly in effort and mental energy, resolves nothing.

This is where systems theory, and especially Rice's model of the self (p. 90), is especially important in helping to define this situation. The effectiveness of the individual lies in knowing the boundary between the self and the outside world and perceiving what is inside and what is outside. Projection blurs this boundary and distorts reality by making what is inside (within the self) appear to be outside. As long as this happens, not only is energy wasted but the internal state of the individual remains unaffected. Action is based on unreality and facts are distorted.

In the same way, Bion explained much of the behaviour of people in groups. The effective group is one that is in contact with reality and knows the boundary between what is inside the group and what is outside. The group becomes ineffective when, through projection techniques, it blurs this boundary and projects its own internal problems on to others. As long as this happens, the group's energy is dissipated and it only regains its effectiveness by realizing that the source of its anxiety is within the group and not outside.

Social defences against anxiety

So far, it has been shown that one important aspect of behaviour is the way in which individuals and groups deal with anxiety, whether the source of danger is a real and external threat to the person or whether it is neurotic, arising from within the self. In the latter case, the ego defends itself by externalizing what is in fact internal by projection.

Bion has shown that in a group, the basic explanation of group action lies in consolidated individual behaviour resulting from the interconnection of individual projection processes. If this is so, then the same sorts of processes should be apparent in society and organizations, and there should be evidence to show that individual mechanisms of defence result in certain social processes and behaviour.

Just as there are ego defences against anxiety, there should be social defences, showing a two-way influence between structure and people. The structure of organizations and society could, presumably, be used by individuals as defences against anxiety and, in turn, these structures could be formed and modified by individual defence mechanisms.

Social defence systems — Jaques' hypothesis

Jaques explored this idea, having been impressed by 'how much institutions are used by individual members to reinforce individual mechanisms of defence against anxiety and in particular against recurrence of the early paranoid and depressive anxieties described by Melanie Klein' (Jaques 1955: 478).

His specific hypothesis postulates that within the life of an organization the defence against anxiety is one of the primary elements that bind the individuals together. In other words, he suggested that within the organization maladaptive behaviour, such as hostility and suspicion, will be exhibited, which is the social counterpart of the symptoms that an individual might exhibit through projection. 'In this sense, individuals may be thought of as externalising those impulses and internal objects that would otherwise give rise to psychotic anxiety and pooling them in the life of the social institutions in which they associate' (Jaques 1955: 479).

Following Klein's theory, anxiety can be classified in the categories of paranoid anxiety and depressive anxiety and social mechanisms of defence against anxiety can be analysed by considering how these are dealt with in a variety of situations.

Defences against paranoid anxiety. According to Klein the anxiety experienced by the infant in its first few months of life is dealt with by the mechanisms of splitting and projective identification. The internal persecutory anxiety is projected on to the breast, which is then experienced as both an external and internal threatening bad object. Jaques theorized that the same defence mechanism is used by individuals in an organization who project their bad internal objects and impulses into a member of that organization who, either by unconscious selection or choice, introjects and absorbs them. An illustration of this process is the role given and taken by the First Officer of a ship. By common consent the First Officer is held to be the source of most of the problems on the ship, including those things for which he is not officially responsible. Jaques suggests that the rest of the crew project their internal bad objects and impulses on to the First Officer and this gives them unconscious relief from their internal persecutors. At the same time, it allows the Captain to be retained as a good protective figure.

Another illustration Jaques gives is that of a nation at war. Here, the citizens project all their bad objects and impulses on to the enemy, so that their internal anxiety is converted (through projection) into fear of an external threat, a real enemy who actually attacks and can be attacked. At the same time, the citizens' hostile and destructive impulses are projected on to their own army, who introject them and then deflect them against the enemy.

The result is that members of the public avoid the guilt of their unconscious hatred and destructive impulses through their socially sanctioned hatred of the enemy. They can now consciously express these impulses in what is considered to be patriotic behaviour against a common foe.

If Jaques's theory is correct, then a nation starting war as an aggressor should reveal an internal situation that is causing its citizens feelings of intense paranoid and persecutory anxiety. Certainly in the current economic crisis in Britain, there is a frequent comparison made between the evident lack of cohesion in the nation now, compared to the *esprit de corps* of wartime Britain. While no-one consciously wants a war to commence it could be argued that there is an unconscious wish for an external enemy on whom citizens could project their hatred and destructive impulses. It is hoped that the black immigrant community will not become the target for these impulses.

Defences against depressive anxiety. According to Klein, the infantile depressive position is characterized by the realization that the good and bad objects are, in fact, aspects of the same thing, that is, the mother can be both good and bad. As well as this, the infant begins to realize that he himself can both love and hate the same object and experiences guilt and despair at his apparent destruction of the loved object.

In adults, situations of persecutory anxiety can cause them to resort to defence mechanisms of this type in order to preserve an internal world of good and bad objects and prevent the anxiety of realizing that both are aspects of the self. Jaques illustrates this situation in terms of social defence with the phenomenon of a majority group scapegoating a minority. Seen from a perspective of the community at large, the community is split into a good majority group scapegoating a minority. Seen from the perspective and preservation of an inner world of good and bad objects.

The majority preserves its belief in its own good by splitting off its own bad parts and feelings, and projecting them on to the minority group. This is revealed in the contempt that it heaps on to the minority and the way it attacks it, reinforced by the cohesiveness of the members of the majority group through intro-jective identification. The clearest example of this must be the way in which the Nazis treated the Jews (although, of course, there were many other factors — social and economic — involved). Central to the Nazi belief was racial purity, which is a genetic myth for any nation, especially for Germany that is the amalga-mation of so many different peoples and cultures. The uncon-scious hatred of the internal impurities, whether racial or per-sonal, were then split off and projected into a clearly visible minority, who could be attacked, abused, and exterminated in the manner in which the individuals would have liked to have treated that part of themselves.

Yet why are some minorities selected for persecution, while others are not? Jaques says that in some way there is a collusion between persecutor and persecuted. In fact, the persecuted minority have a precise and equally strong hatred of the majority.

'In view of the selective factor in choice of persecuted minori-ties, we must consider the possibility that one of the operative factors in this selection is the consensus in the minority group,

at the phantasy level, to seek contempt and suffering in order
to alleviate unconscious guilt.'   (Jaques 1955: 486)

An illustration from industry. Jaques then presented an illustration based on his own experience gained when working with
Glacier Metals, a small engineering company on the outskirts of
London (Jaques 1951). As a consultant to that organization, he
experienced negotiations that were taking place between management and a team of shop-floor representatives concerning the
abolition of the piece-work payment system. The negotiations and
discussions took place over a seven-month period and revealed
certain contradictory attitudes. While the discussions took place
in a friendly atmosphere, there were many incidents that revealed
the workers' intense suspicion of management and this was shown
by the length of the negotiations. At the same time, management
frequently expressed their confidence in the responsibility of the
workers, in spite of apparent evidence to the contrary.

An analysis of this situation, based on the operation of social
defences against anxiety, helps to explain the great difficulties
encountered in the negotiations despite the good labour relations
and high morale of the company. Jaques suggests that the workers
had unconsciously split the management into good and bad, the
'good' managers being the ones they worked with daily, and the
'bad' ones being those with whom they negotiated. By projecting
their good impulses into the managers in the work situation they
were able to maintain good working relations with them. However, the workers' hostile and destructive impulses were projected
on to their representatives who then deflected them against the
'bad' managers in the negotiating situation. In this way, the
representatives were able to feel an external social sanction for
their suspicion and hostility in the sense that they could feel that
these bad impulses did not belong to them, but to the people they
represented.

The idealization of the workers by the management, revealed
by the reiteration of the view that they (the workers) could be
expected to do their part responsibly, is explained by the mechanism of idealization, splitting, and denial. Managers split off the
good and bad aspects of their own management control, projecting on to the workers the good aspects, seeing them as

responsible people, and idealizing them into perfect workers. By denying the bad aspects of the workers, they were in fact denying their own bad aspects and hence placating and defending them-selves from their own internal persecutors.

Thus the attitude of workers and management, expressed through the various defence mechanisms, complemented and reinforced each other, and this developed into a circular process. The more the representatives attacked the managers, the more the managers idealized them in order to placate them. 'The greater the concessions given by management to the workers, the greater was the guilt and fear of depressive anxiety in the workers and hence the greater the retreat to paranoid attitudes as a means of avoiding depressive anxiety' (Jaques 1955: 493).

Social defence systems — a hospital case study

The purpose of Jaques's paper was to test the hypothesis that one of the primary forces that cause the cohesion of people in organi-zations is their defence against anxiety, with the converse that organizations are used by individual members as defence mechanisms against their own anxieties.

This idea was taken up and used by Menzies in her study of the nursing service of a general hospital (Menzies 1970). The hospital, a large London teaching hospital with approximately 700 beds, had 700 nurses of whom about 550 were student nurses. The problem presented to Menzies concerned the allocation of the student nurses to meet the staffing needs of the hospital, while at the same time attempting to give the nurses appropriate experi-ence for their professional training. Menzies's help was requested to prevent what was felt by the senior staff to be an impending breakdown in this system of allocation. She described her relation-ship with the hospital as 'socio-therapeutic' in which the aim was to facilitate desired social change.

Through her analytic experience, Menzies regarded this situa-tion as the 'presenting' problem, that is, a problem that can be openly expressed as socially acceptable, but which is in fact a sympton of the real underlying problem that can only be uncovered by hard work between analyst and client. This diagnos-tic work was carried out by intensive interviews and discussions both formal and informal. These discussions revealed that the major factor in the situation was the high level of tension, distress, and anxiety shown by the nurses. 'We found it hard to understand how nurses could tolerate so much anxiety, and indeed we found much evidence that they could not.' (Menzies 1970: 3). Sickness ratios were high and in fact one third of all the student nurses failed to complete their training, the majority withdrawing at their own request. From this diagnosis, Menzies analysed and studied the cause and nature of this anxiety.

Nature of the anxiety.   No matter how well a hospital is organized, the nature of a nurse's work is likely to arouse a great deal of anxiety and other emotions. The jobs she has to perform are frequently frightening and disgusting. Intimate contact with patients may arouse libidinal desires and in spite of loving and caring attention, a patient may die. Both patients and relatives will have a variety of conflicting emotions towards the nurse, such as gratitude for the care and attention received, envy of her skills and health, and hostility at their enforced dependence on her. According to Menzies, this confused and highly emotional situation confronting the nurse, 'bears a striking resemblance to the phantasy situations that exist in every individual in the deepest and most primitive levels of the mind' (Menzies 1970: 5). Through the pressure of these intense and persecutory anxieties generated through her work, the nurse projects her unconscious infantile phantasy situations into her work situation and then re-experiences all the vivid and painful emotions that are really appropriate to the phantasies. These violent and intense feelings, which Klein has shown to be present in the infant's phantasy life, are then experienced as part of the nurse's adult life.

Of course, early attitudes and experiences affect every adult's life, and problems of relationships that remain unresolved in infancy are frequently revived in a modified form. As Klein said: 'the attitude towards a subordinate or a superior repeats up to a point the relation to a young sibling or to a parent ... A condescending and unpleasant older individual stirs up anew the rebellious attitudes of a child towards his parents' (Klein 1959: 299).

The nurse, by projecting her phantasy situations into the work situations uses this universal technique for mastering anxiety. The objective situation is used as a 'symbolic representation' of the inner phantasy situation and, in as far as the objective work situation is mastered, then symbolically the phantasy situation is mastered, leading to internal reassurance and a diminution of anxiety. However, problems arise when the objective situation does not symbolically represent an inner phantasy, but is equated with it. When this happens (and Menzies believed this was happening to the nurses) the symbol fails to contain the anxiety, but in fact causes it. The result is that in the work situation 'nurses will consequently experience the full force of their primitive infantile anxieties in consciousness' (Menzies 1970: 9). The work situation, instead of providing a legitimate and essential opportunity for the individual to cope, and develop skills to deal, with anxiety, was in fact causing the nurses to regress.

Defensive techniques. Menzies argued (following Jaques) that one of the factors in any organization that helps determine its structure, culture, and mode of functioning is the social defence system. This is the result of the collusion between each member of the organization as they attempt to operate their own psychic defence mechanism. Menzies gave many examples of the operation of the social defence system. For instance, decision-making can clearly be a life and death matter in a hospital and could cause a great deal of stress and anxiety. The defence against this anxiety is what Menzies called 'ritual task performance'. Each nurse was taught to work by following an extremely rigid task-list, and the attitude inculcated was that every task is a matter of life and death, to be treated with appropriate seriousness. Consequently, student nurses were actively discouraged from using their discretion and initiative.

Perhaps the most interesting illustration of the hospital's social defence system was the way in which nurses attempted to minimize their anxiety regarding their individual responsibility. Each nurse experienced a powerful internal conflict between the responsibility demanded by her work and her wishes to avoid this heavy and continuous burden by acting irresponsibly. This conflict was partially avoided by the processes of denial, splitting, and projection, which converted this intra-personal struggle into an interpersonal conflict. 'Each nurse tends to split off aspects of herself from her conscious personality and to project them into other nurses' (Menzies 1970: 17).

The irresponsible impulses were projected into a nurse's subordinate, who was then treated with the severity which that part of the split-off self deserved. The stern and harsh aspects of herself were split off and projected into her superiors so that she expected harsh disciplinary treatment from them. The formation of these psychic roles was clearly seen in the hospital when nurses habitually claimed that other nurses were careless, irresponsible, and in need of continual supervision and discipline. This clearly illustrates how part of the culture and operation of the hospital resulted from the social defence system, arising from the individual seeking relief from the anxiety caused by internal persecutors. Other examples of the social defence system revealed ways in which individuality was minimized, both for nurses and patients so that feelings of attachment could be denied.

Defences against anxiety are at the same time defences against reality, when the external or internal situations present a stress situation too painful to bear, and the individual regresses to primitive psychic defence mechanisms. In organizations, this is revealed in social defence systems that help individuals avoid the feelings of anxiety, guilt, and uncertainty. However, because these defences require energy to operate them, it follows that there must be less available energy for the primary task. At the individual level, the ego is weakened when mechanisms of splitting, projection, and denial are employed. Bion has shown that at the group level, the work group ceases to operate when anxiety and other emotions cause the group to work in one of the basic assumption modes. The way forward is to enable the individual to 'work through' their anxieties by facing and coming to terms with the cause of them, that is, by facing reality. Yet Menzies found that in the hospital, although 'anxiety is to some extent contained, true mastery of anxiety by deep working-through and modification is seriously inhibited. Thus, it is to be expected that nurses will persistently experience a higher degree of anxiety than is justified by the objective situation alone' (Menzies 1970: 25).

The social defence system not only failed to alleviate primary anxiety but also caused secondary anxiety. For instance, the fixed, ritual-like procedures for carrying out tasks made it impossible for the nurses to adjust to varying work loads, which led to a constant fear of an impending crisis. The constant movement of nurses from one position to another, seen by Menzies as a defence against close individual relationships, caused anxiety due to the requirements of the new and unknown situation. Staff levels, always planned for peak loads, and the way in which the nurses' work was allocated, resulted in guilty feelings of underemployment and job dissatisfaction.

Although the social defence system in the hospital developed originally from the combination of each individual's need, it rapidly became fixed and rigid. Because of the nursing profession's unwillingness to change, each new student was forced to accept the norms that had developed and she was unable to project her own psychic defences into the social system and contribute to and modify it. She was forced to introject the hospital's defence system and this resulted in the new student experiencing a considerable degree of pathological anxiety. Menzies's conclusion was bleak. The hospital system was not only failing to develop the nurses' ability to recognize and deal with anxiety but 'in many cases it forces the individual to regress to a maturation level below that which she had achieved before she entered the hospital' (Menzies 1970: 36).

A case study of residential institutions

A further example of social defences against anxiety is given by Miller and Gwynne in their pilot study of residential institutions for the physically handicapped and the young chronic sick (Miller and Gwynne 1972). This study illustrates how anxiety arises from the task that society gives to institutions of this sort, such as the Cheshire Home. 'The task that society assigns — behaviourally though never verbally — to these institutions is to cater for the socially dead during the interval between social death and physical death' (Miller and Gwynne 1972: 80). Carrying out such a grim and painful task must inevitably create intense stress and anxiety, which affects not only the staff but also the inmates. The authors analyse the culture and practice of such institutions in terms of social defence mechanisms.

These defences are divided into two categories, namely the humanitarian defence and the liberal defence. The humanitarian defence is based on humanitarian values, prolonging life at all costs but without asking for what purpose. Society wants to believe that the inmates are happy and contented and is affronted by any show of discontent, which is equated with ingratitude. The liberal defence attempts to deny the inmates' abnormalities and fosters the myth that they are really normal. Hopes are encouraged of physical cures and social rehabilitation, which any inmate realizes are false as soon as he attempts to cross the boundary into 'normal' society. Staff professing these liberal values frequently infantalize the inmates by saying that 'they are just like children'.

Resulting from these defences are two models of residential care, the differences arising from the different perceptions of the primary task. The first is the 'warehouse' model, in which the task is perceived to be the prolonging of physical life. An institution using this model concentrates on the provision of medical and nursing care and the 'good' inmate is the one who accepts the staff's diagnosis and treatment of his needs.

The other is the 'horticultural' model in which the primary task is the development of the deprived individual's unfulfilled capacities. Although the latter model would seem to result in greater advantages for the individual inmate, both are in fact social defence mechanisms 'set up to cope with the intolerable anxieties that are associated with the task that society implicitly defines for these institutions'. The real task for these institutions is to help the inmates make their transition from social death to physical death by providing a setting in which they can find their own best way of relating to themselves and to the environment.

Institutional defences. Like Menzies's study of the hospital, Miller and Gwynne found the operation of a social defence against close staff/inmate relationships. There was usually a duty roster, which ensured that staff rotated their duties with different inmates, which preserved an interpersonal distance. The inmates, especially in institutions operating the warehouse model, were depersonalized and non-differentiated by being treated as either mentally incompetent, or as if they were all as totally crippled as an advanced sclerotic. This defended the staff against the varied needs and abilities (albeit limited) of individuals. A similar defence was seen in some institutions in the attitude of staff to aids and equipment, such as electric wheelchairs. These were usually dismissed as irrelevant and useless toys, perhaps because 'staff who reject aids, whether on the ground of expense or that their inmates are too helpless to manage them, are really expressing an inability to tolerate a measure of independence in those they look after' (Miller and Gwynne 1972: 133).

Other social defence mechanisms arose because of the inevitable death of the inmates. Using general systems theory, an institution caring for the chronic disabled has only one export, and that is dead inmates, and this is bound to cause intense anxiety among the staff. While some defences must be inevitable and to some extent essential, nevertheless energy devoted to such defences could be channeled into greater care for the inmates. It was found that inmates were frequently transferred to other institutions when they showed signs of physical or mental deterioration. Some institutions took in a small number of people in a different category of illness, either those convalescing or those with a terminal illness. It can be supposed that the motive for the former action was the hope that the incurables might gain comfort from the convalescents, and the latter a sense of gratitude and relative fortune from the incurables. A further defence mechanism, and perhaps the one having the greatest effect on these institutions, was the assumption that the critical import-export process involved the staff rather than the inmates. This is a defence against paranoid anxiety, whereby the inmates and the staff split off their bad objects and feelings and projected them in to a suitable member of staff. Miller and Gwynne found that in every institution at least one staff member was considered at best incompetent and unsympathetic, and at worst sadistic. Alongside this, some staff were idealized as always good and benign. This process could escalate into the belief that all the troubles and problems of the institution would go away if only the bad and wicked matron would leave. The proof that this mechanism actually operates is seen in the staff wastage figures — over 30 per cent per annum, with a higher turnover for the heads of these types of institution than others. Inevitably, after a while, the new replacement, seen initially as all that is good, falls from grace and the process is likely to begin all over again.

The counterpart of this mechanism was also observed — the

scapegoating of inmates by the staff. The assumption arose that the home would be a better place if only a certain patient would leave, and sometimes this assumption was turned into reality by an inmate being consigned to a mental hospital.

To complete their study, Miller and Gwynne make some tentative suggestions for better organization and leadership of these institutions, which avoid the pitfalls of the warehouse and horticultural models. They recognize three sub-systems that should operate within the total management of the institution.

Dependence system This deals with the physical resources needed to help the inmates cope with their daily living activities, such as dressing, feeding, and so forth. However, this cannot be the only operating system, otherwise the inmates have no role, other than to be dressed and fed, which is in fact what happens in institutions operating the warehouse model.

Independence system The primary task of this system is to provide an environment that gives the inmates opportunities to act

Figure 11 The basic organizational model

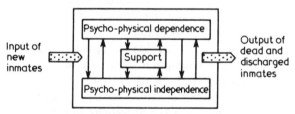

The institution as an open system, showing constituent systems of activities

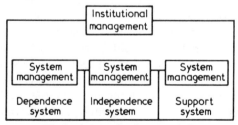

The basic organizational model

Source: Miller and Gwynne (1972: 190)

as independent individuals. These opportunities may result in what may seem trivial activities to the normal person, that is, delivering the letters, and may be taken up by only a few. Nevertheless, it allows the inmates to manage, to some extent, their own personal boundaries.

Support system   This system, an innovation, would provide a counselling service, perhaps backed up by external psychiatric resources although local voluntary services, such as the church, could make a valid contribution.

The institution is an open system, and an organizational model, based on the three sub-systems illustrated in *Figure 11*.

10 Mental energy, anxiety, and effectiveness

The preceding chapters have ranged over a wide variety of theory and practice, illustrating the influence that psychoanalytic theory has had on understanding the way people behave in groups and organizations. The work of some of the significant people in this field shows a clear link in the chain of development of thought, which is most clearly illustrated by the progression of ideas that originated with Freud and then developed by Klein and Bion. However, other chapters show a less obvious link. For instance, there is no immediate connection between Klein's theories of the early development of an infant and Trist's studies of coal-miners. Or what is the link between T-groups and Menzies's study of social defence systems in a hospital? It is the aim of this book to show that all of this work has been influenced in some way by psychoanalysis, but the question remains, in what particular way?

The concept of mental energy

The answer, I believe, lies in the concept of mental energy and the ways in which this energy is distributed and used. Mental energy powers the psychic apparatus; the part of the mind that processes information received through the senses and that then results in physical activity. In a baby, the psychic apparatus is primitive and the mental energy, which is continually generated by the instincts, is used up almost immediately in muscular activity. However, as an individual develops, so also do the various systems within this apparatus, such as memory, perception, and the ability to create and manipulate ideas. Consequently, mental energy begins to flow into and power these parts of the psychic apparatus. This energy is no longer immediately dissipated through action, but can be used to delay action through thinking or can block it entirely through repression. A memory, a perception, or an idea only gains significance for an individual when the psychic apparatus invests it with a charge of energy. A person is constantly surrounded by a vast number of stimuli, which he perceives through his senses, only some of which become significant. Some stimuli may act directly on the emotions, others may trigger off memories and associations, and some may be perceived to offer personal advantage. For whatever reason, their significance to the individual results from the fact that they become charged with energy and have power within the mental system to affect behaviour.

The psychic apparatus is the means by which mental energy, constantly generated through the instincts, is distributed and allocated throughout the total personality. The observable results are seen in the behaviour displayed by each individual, but equally important are the memories and ideas that remain within the personality but that are now charged with energy and are capable of being activated by appropriate stimuli.

This concept of mental energy is central to Freud's dynamic theory of personality and is called cathexis.* An object (or more precisely the mental perception of an object) is said to be cathected when it has a charge of mental energy invested in it. Most important, when an idea or memory is cathected, it is energized and has the power and drive to affect behaviour, either immediately or in the future.

Once a perception is cathected, it retains its power to affect action and thought indefinitely. For instance, old people retain the power to recall their childhood memories in detail, although they may forget what they did on the previous day. An illustration of the enduring power of cathected concepts is shown by Proust's autobiographical novel *A la Recherche du Temps Perdu*. His detailed recollections of childhood were triggered off by the memories caused by eating a madelaine, which was the type of cake he ate as a boy.

The total amount of mental energy available at any one time is

*The term 'cathexis' is a translation of the original German 'Besetzung' which means 'investment'.

finite and therefore the investment of energy in one particular mental process means that less is available for any other. For instance, a particular memory or association may be cathected but if it is considered dangerous or painful, it may be repressed into the unconscious. As an equal amount of energy must be used to keep it repressed so less is available for other mental work. Consequently a person's behaviour may show abnormalities, such as the inability to cope with normal situations due to the lack of mental energy available. Freud gave many examples where repression is the indirect cause of pathological behaviour (Freud 1974).

Defences against anxiety

The mature, coping adult is one who can interact with other people and satisfy his needs in ways that are acceptable to himself and to society. However, the environment is not always benign and in order to survive, every person develops techniques for dealing with danger. A person is aware of danger through experiencing the feeling of anxiety. As stated earlier, anxiety is especially significant among all other unpleasant feelings, because it causes automatic bodily responses, such as an increased pulse-rate, faster breathing, and so forth.

Anxiety may be caused by an external dangerous situation or by an internal perception of danger. Either way, a person feels threatened and attempts to rid himself of the threat. If the danger is external, it can be dealt with either by avoidance or by mastering and overcoming it. In fact, the physiological changes such as increased pulse-rate, are autonomous mechanisms designed to aid the physical activity of fight or flight. However, the situation is different when anxiety is caused by a perception of danger that originates in the inner world of the self. Every individual develops techniques for dealing with this neurotic anxiety and these are called the ego defences.

The most usual defence against this internal anxiety is called projection, where for instance the feeling 'I hate you' is transformed by projection into the anxiety-reducing feeling 'You hate me'. Subject and object have been changed and because the threat is now externalized, action can be taken. As Hall and Lindzey wrote:

'If one remembers that on the whole the ego is better prepared by experience and practice to deal with external dangers, it is easy to see why projection is such a prevalent defense. By fabricating a 'real' enemy, the person feels adequate to take command of the situation. He can, for example, destroy or attempt to destroy his enemy: this allows him to satisfy his aggressive impulse without incurring a feeling of shame. For this reason, projection is probably the most effective of the defense mechanisms.'   (Hall and Lindzey 1968: 271)

But this defence offers no permanent solution since the person continues to carry the danger around with him and nothing is resolved. In terms of mental energy, projection involves transferring a cathexis involving a perception of the self to one involving a perception of an external object. To the extent that this happens, contact with reality is lost. The feeling of anxiety is temporarily reduced, which is the object of the exercise, but the consequence is that energy, both mental and physical, is used to attack a 'straw man'. The source of the anxiety still remains within the mental system although psychic and physical resources have been depleted in the process.

In other words, work has been done involving action, feelings, and emotions, but nothing has changed as a result. It can now be seen why Klein's theory of projective identification (which is one specific form of projection) is so central to her work and also forms the nucleus of Bion's theories of groups. Processes of projection are the most frequent ways in which individuals and groups lose their effectiveness. Their energy, first mental and then physical is spent on work that is essentially a phantasy and a delusion. In order for the situation to be resolved successfully, the root cause of the anxiety must be recognized as being located not outside but within, and this requires not only self-knowledge of a high order, but also an ego strong enough to deal with the real cause.

The amount of projection that an individual uses depends on two factors. One is his personal propensity to use this defence mechanism, and is an aspect of personality. For instance, in a T-group, where structure and organization are reduced to a minimum, people begin to understand their own propensity to react to anxiety by projection. Yet this self-knowledge cannot by itself ensure that the same person, when working in an organization, will continue to minimize projection and hostility. For the other factor that affects projection is the situation in which the person exists. At work the social structure of the organization creates a climate that either fosters or reduces feelings of anxiety and therefore directly affects the likelihood that a person will feel threatened and resort to projection. As Jaques said:

> 'It is not my intention to suggest that social tension and mistrust are merely psycho-pathological phenomena, and that if everyone were psychoanalysed then social disruption and destructive conflict would disappear. However free from psychopathological suspicion the members of a society might be, they will have to discover how to design their social institutions to enable individual constructiveness to express itself.'

> (Jaques 1976: 7)

Therefore Rice's and Trists's studies help to reveal the factors in work, such as the nature of the task and the structure of the organization, that directly affect the level of anxiety felt by the workers and hence the amount of energy that will be used in defence mechanisms.

The more threatening the external situation, the more likely a person will resort to projection. Work and organizational design must therefore aim to create a working environment where mental energy can be used in the performance of the task and where danger can be recognized and mastered by legitimate and useful work. Otherwise groups and even the total organization can resort to projection and waste their energy in aggression and hostility.

Perhaps another way of putting this is to say that, for the individual, the ideal situation is one where external reality can be perceived and where, at the same time, psychic reality can be acknowledged.

Freud and mental energy

Freud believed that the group or organization is bonded by libidinal energy, initially focused on the leader. Through the process of identification, the leader is introjected into the ego-ideal of each individual member and this enables the members to identify with each other. What Freud did not consider was what happens when the leader makes demands on the group by asking them to do something. When this happens the members must allocate mental energy to the task and therefore less is available for affective bonds between each other and the leader. In an extreme example, the libidinal bond may be so strong that members will follow the leader even if this means death, such as Christian martyrdom. However, immediately a leader makes task demands of his group, his position is potentially in danger and the group is liable to break up. Unless additional energy is available from the group the leader must import energy from outside, which can then be used to maintain and strengthen his position. The tyrant or dictator, who may have gained his position initially through the love of his followers, must create military force and armed guards to preserve himself in power.

The other way of preserving leadership is the paradox of ensuring that the leader makes no task demands. An example of this is modern democratic royalty, such as the British monarchy, where the Queen has no executive power and can make no task demands on the nation. Consequently she can be the object of loving feelings and the focus of patriotism and loyalty. The libidinal energy, focused on to her results in many citizens feeling affective ties between themselves. However, the head of the executive, that is, the Prime Minister, because he must make demands of the citizens, is rarely loved and can be the focus of intense dislike and hostility. Nevertheless, he is maintained in power through the libidinal energy of the majority of the electorate and if that diminishes, an election is called.

In contrast, the American presidency combines both symbolic and executive leadership and any presidential task-demands immediately lessens the libidinal energy available for bonding with the president and between the citizens. It is interesting to note that during the 1976 American presidential elections, the leading candidates minimized their policy statements (which would have involved task demands) thereby attempting to diminish any obstacles to the formation of libidinal ties between themselves and the electorate.

Klein

Klein's description of the earliest mental processes in the infant are essentially attempts to describe how mental energy arises and how it is distributed. In her model of behaviour, the infant's only initial reality is the mother's breast and therefore all its primitive feelings and emotions are related to what the breast provides or fails to provide. Klein pictured a mental state of extremes, of love or hate, and of paranoid terror or blissful satiation. In the initial paranoid-schizoid position the infant continually engages and withdraws from reality, and uses its mental energy in the twin processes of introjective and projective identification. If the mother provides loving care, then the infant needs to invest less energy into the splitting processes (which are needed to keep the good and bad apart) and can invest more energy into its libidinal drives, resulting in loving feelings and reparative acts towards the mother.

What is then established as the basic patterns of behaviour are the twin mechanisms of projective and introjective identification as defences against persecutory anxiety. Mental energy, which could be used to engage and deal with the external reality, is withdrawn and invested in these processes as a defence against internal anxiety.

When this happens, the perceived bad parts of the self are no longer able to be accepted internally and are violently expelled and projected into other people, who are then perceived as bad and threatening. However, using the concept of finite energy, the mental energy used in this process of defence means a weakening of the ego. As an extreme example, the chronic paranoid is unable to live normally in society because all his mental energy is used to defend himself from his persecutors, which he perceives as external enemies but which are in fact internal. Likewise the schizophrenic uses all his energy to keep apart the opposing aspects of himself which he cannot reconcile. Consequently he is likely to withdraw more and more from the real world, having no energy left for engagement with reality. At a less extreme level one of the symptoms of depression, whether reactive or endogenous, is tiredness. This can be explained by the idea that mental energy is being used internally in defence processes and little remains for normal activity.

Bion

Bion's great contribution was to make these unconscious projection processes central to group life, and his theory essentially deals with the distribution of mental energy within a group. When the group operates in the mode of the work group, all its energy is concentrated on dealing with the task. This means that the group is engaging with reality, which involves the demands of the task, the constantly changing pressures of the environment, and the problems of individuals working in co-operation with each other.

When the group feels threatened, anxiety causes it to withdraw energy from dealing with the task and to use it to defend itself against these anxieties. When it does this, the group moves into the basic assumption modes and operates in the manner of pairing, fight/flight, or dependency. However, because the mental energy of the group is now being used in these defences, no work can be done and no development can take place. Just as the individual ego is weakened when its energies are deployed in defence, so the group is weakened when it moves into one of the basic assumptions. Perhaps one of the clearest illustrations of an organization currently working in the basic assumption mode is shown by the British car industry. A large part of its energy is being used in internal fighting and this weakens its ability to compete against foreign competition. This results in a vicious circle, whereby the increasing influx of foreign cars creates even more anxiety, which is revealed in further strikes and stoppages. The eventual panic that is now being felt is unlikely to cease until drastic organizational changes can redirect the energy back to the task. Failing that, the organization will cease to operate.

Menzies's words, although written to describe a hospital situation, seem appropriate: 'It is unfortunately true of the paranoid-schizoid defence systems that they prevent true insights into the nature of problems and realistic appreciation of their seriousness. Thus, only too often, no action can be taken until a crisis is very near or has actually occurred' (Menzies 1970: 42).

Bion's model of group activity has three essential and basic differences to Freud's approach. The first is that, for Bion, the bonding in the group is not necessarily libidinal. It may be so when the group is in the basic assumption mode of pairing, for contained in that mode is the assumption that the pair have formed for the sexual purpose of procreation — whether to produce the hoped-for Messiah or the saving idea. In fact, Bion says that Freud's theory emerged from the psychoanalytic pairing of analyst and patient where bonding was essentially libidinal.

However in the other two basic assumption modes, fight/flight and dependency, the bonding in the group comes not from libidinal ties, but from the leader who is the common focus for the group's projective identification. In either of those two modes, the group members do not need to like each other, but only to feel that the same leader can save them from their own fears.

The second difference, for Bion, is that the leader in the basic assumption modes is created by the group and is the creature of the group. His power comes from the energy invested in him by the group, which is limited and directional. The leader leads only as long as he unconsciously colludes with the group's demands, which are not task-directed but defence mechanisms designed to protect them from their internal anxieties. As soon as he fails to do this, he is deposed or ignored, or else he has to invest huge amounts of energy to maintain his position. Either way, energy is used to maintain some sort of equilibrium within the group, but with increased tension. Little or no energy is available to engage with reality and the group feeds on itself. Unless some action is taken to face the real anxieties and deal appropriately with them, the group faces disaster either by being torn apart or by coming to a complete halt.

The third difference from Freud in Bion's model is that the latter believed the underlying processes in groups are those described by Klein as being operative in the earliest development stages of the infant's life. When the group faces persecutory anxiety, then the individual members unconsciously collude with one another in the processes of splitting and projective identification. Because of physical proximity and the common experience of a shared 'climate', the group provides the ideal setting for projective and introjective identification. When the group shares a common anxiety, the individual processes illustrated by Klein are more likely to be focused on one person. What is simply a feeling of dislike between two people can become transposed in the group situation into the phenomenon of scapegoating. Similarly, the feeling of admiration between two people, can result in the election of the dependent group leader. The group setting allows and encourages the channelling of the members' mental energy on to a focal person. Of course, the focal person must give some indication that he can carry the role directed towards him. It may well be that this accounts for the many flawed and psychologically misbalanced people who have held high office in state, war, and industry. It is precisely their flaws and imperfections that encourage their followers to identify with, and project, on to them. The evenly balanced man is unlikely to give those signs that encourage projection, or if it happens, he is more likely to be aware of what is happening and reject the projected role.

Lewin

Lewin's ideas and theories are self-evidently concerned with psychological forces, their interaction and effect. He never described them as 'mental', but his concept of 'life space' as being the psychological field of forces in which each individual exists, and especially his emphasis on the subjective nature of this field clearly deals with the same phenomenon. Lewin emphasized the importance of the interrelationship between the forces acting on the individual from outside and the individual himself, so that implicit in all his work is the concept of mental energy. For instance, in his early work in Germany with Zeigarnick, the preferential recall of unfinished tasks was explained by the fact that mental energy (called 'tension' by Lewin) was associated with the unfinished tasks, that is, they were cathected, while the energy associated with the finished tasks had been dissipated in their completion and no longer had energy associated with them.

Lewin used his field theory to explain the physical outcome of the equilibrium established between the psychological driving and restraining forces in any situation. He saw the production level in a factory as the equilibrium point resulting from these two opposing sets of psychological forces. In this model, the production level can rise through either an increase in the driving forces or a reduction in the restraining forces. It was his belief that an increase in the driving forces increased psychological tension and this resulted in increased fatigue and aggressiveness. In other words (although Lewin did not say this) the situation would generate anxiety and encourage projection. He believed that his group approach resulted in higher output through a reduction in the restraining forces. His model allows the interpretation that a reduction of the restraining forces makes more mental energy available which can be used, not only in carrying out the task, but in creative thinking about the way in which the task can be done. That is to say, by the participation of individuals in the decision-making process, as illustrated by Lewin's 'food-habits' experiments or the pacing cards in the pyjama factory, individuals invest a certain amount of mental energy into the decision, that is, they are cathected. The decision is now significant to the individual due to the energy invested in it and leads to its implementation in order for this energy to be discharged. On the other hand, when individuals are merely told what to do, there is no personal investment in the decision, that is, no cathexis occurs, and so no commitment will result.

An understanding of this process helps one to understand how Lewin 'discovered' the laboratory method, because his approach leads from merely description to prescription. When his experiments showed the value of using group decision-making processes, it implied that these could be used to increase personal and organizational effectiveness generally. While the boundary is far from exact, Lewin showed that groups could be used for educative as well as therapeutic purposes.

General systems theory

Because general systems theory originated in the field of physics it is by definition dealing with energy, its transfer and distribution. When applied to living systems it illuminates the subject by showing that what is apparently static is in fact in a state of dynamic equilibrium with continual change.

When this concept of open systems is applied to the individual, it is seen that a person operates normally as long as the ego defines the boundary between what is inside and what is outside, and controls the transactions between the one and the other. Hence the individual must have sufficient mental energy available to enable the ego to function effectively. If the person is under intense anxiety, then this energy is withdrawn and invested into various defence mechanisms. In other words, the person ceases to operate as an open system and works as a closed system in as far as the boundary control function of the ego ceases to operate. However, the external forces from the outside world continue to impinge on the person and unless he can divert energy to deal with them, he will malfunction and behave abnormally.

When open systems theory is applied to groups and organizations, it illuminates in particular the role of management. The organization is then seen to be a living system, open to and in contact with its environment, where the essential need is for work to be done at the boundaries, so that appropriate exchanges can be made across the boundary, thereby maintaining the organization in a state of dynamic equilibrium with its environment. This is a management function and requires a large investment of the organization's mental energy to react and proact with all the variety of forces arising from society, government, competitors, and the economy in general.

However, the work of continually monitoring and reacting with the environment, and maintaining an appropriate internal organization, is an energy-consuming task that can create intense anxieties. If, for instance, an old-established family firm realizes that its product and methods are no longer appropriate to the 1970s, the anxiety may be so strong that energy is withdrawn from managing the boundary and used in a whole variety of defence mechanisms to avoid the real issue. For a time these will protect the firm from the need to change and adapt, but unless it eventually faces up to this harsh reality, it will inevitably go bankrupt.

The withdrawal of energy from engagement with reality moves the organization into a closed system, which by definition can do no work. It can now be seen that Bion's basic assumption groups are all closed systems. The anxiety in the organization results in projection processes and energy is used in internal fighting or in the avoidance of real issues. This behaviour not only prevents energy being available for legitimate work, that is, the primary task, but has no effect on the continuing and remorseless impact of the real world.

Social systems as a defence against anxiety

Every individual develops techniques for defending himself against feelings of anxiety. The psychoanalytic approach emphasizes the centrality of the defence techniques in the total spectrum of behaviour, because they are primary causes of personal ineffectiveness. Techniques, such as projection, require the investment of mental energy for their operation and the more they are used, the less energy is available for authentic responses to reality. These defence mechanisms become established within the personality and are significant factors in the behaviour patterns that a person is most likely to follow. In many ways, personality can be considered as the traditional behaviour patterns that a person establishes for himself. The more anxiety he feels, the more likely he is to automatically resort to these traditional ways of behaving, which will include defence techniques.

From an everyday point of view the way in which an organization, such as a factory, develops its structure and method of operation is mainly determined by the product it produces and the technology it uses. However, from a psychological viewpoint, the culture, structure, and mode of functioning are determined by the psychological needs of the members. Because anxiety defence mechanisms are so important in shaping individual behaviour, it follows that they will directly affect social life in organizations. The formation of tradition, the structure of work, and the methods by which people deal with each other will all be influenced by the ways in which anxiety is, and has been, dealt with.

As Menzies wrote:

'The needs of the members of the organisation to use it in the struggle against anxiety leads to the development of socially structured defence mechanisms which appear as elements in the structure, culture and mode of functioning of the organisation. A social defence system develops over time as the result of collusive interaction and agreement, often unconscious, between members of the organisation as to what form it will take. The socially structured defence mechanisms then tend to become an aspect of external reality with which old and new members of the institution must come to terms.'

(Menzies 1970: 10)

This means that traditions and methods of working frequently result from the operation of defence mechanisms and therefore constantly require mental energy for their operation. The energy needed for this activity means that less is available for productive work. Such procedures not only continually draw energy and resources from the organization but also avoid the real causes of anxiety and prevent them from being dealt with effectively. Work can provide opportunities for people to work through and master their anxieties, resulting in psychological growth and an increased ability to take on greater responsibilities. Rigid traditions and inappropriate work methods often lead to psychological stunting or even regression, so that a person's ability to cope with his own anxieties are diminished.

Social defence systems evolve to meet a real need, the need to reduce anxiety. However, because these systems rapidly become institutionalized, it means that newcomers must adapt to them and have little chance to modify or contribute to them. For them, they are inappropriate and so they not only fail to temporarily reduce anxiety, but also can even cause it.

The concept of social defence systems helps one to understand why organizational change is so difficult and so often resisted. Changing an organization automatically means that social defences will be restructured and while this is happening, anxieties are likely to be more open and intense. The opposition and resistance to change can be understood by seeing it as the fear people have of relinquishing established social systems that have helped to defend them against anxiety in the past. The old system will reflect the power and influence the previous generation had to shape the system to fit their own psychological needs. A change inevitably means changes in power and influence, which will be reflected in new ways of operation and consequently new social defence systems. Unless people have the opportunity to participate in the changes they will not be able to influence the formation of new social systems and the result will be an increase in suspicion, hostility, and aggression.

In conclusion, the concept of mental energy emphasizes the enormous potential of power and creativity present in every person and available to organizations that understand the processes of human behaviour.

It remains to be seen whether future managers will have the insights and the courage to create new forms of organization which, for the first time, will enable the full, dynamic humanity of man to operate at work.

Appendix
The life of Kurt Lewin —
a chronology of events

1890   Born in Posen (now in Poland)

1910   Student at Berlin University. Studied with Carl Stumpf, Professor of Psychology. Also philosophy under Ernst Cassirer

1914   Joined German army

1916   Awarded degree in psychology

1918   Demobilized. Worked at Berlin Psychological Institute. Also working there were Köhler and Wertheimer, 'Gestalt' psychologists

1922   Published *The Concept of Genesis (or Origin) in Physics, Biology and Evolutionary History*

1924-31 'Berlin Experiments' with Zeigarnick, *et alia*, concerning tension, anger, and field theory

1927   Appointed associate Professor

1929   Publication by Brown in *American Psychology Review* 'The Methods of Kurt Lewin — a Study of Action and Effort'. First evaluation of Lewin's work in English. Visited Yale — International Congress of Psychology.

1932   Spent six months as visiting Professor at Stanford University

1933   Emigrated to the United States. Worked at Cornell University — Department of Home Economics

1935   Moved to Iowa Child Welfare Research Station

1936   Published *Principles of Topological Psychology*

1938   'Autocracy-Democracy' experiments with Lippitt and White

1939   Bavelas and Harwood Manufacturing Corporation

1940   Became an American citizen. 'Food-habit' studies

1944   Established Research Centre for Group Dynamics at Massachusetts Institute of Technology. (After his death, this moved to Michigan University, Ann Arbor). Launched Commission on Community Interrelations for the American Jewish Congress

1946   Workshop at New Britain, Connecticut. Origin of T-group

1947   (Feb) Died

           (June) First publication of *Human Relations*. First article was 'Frontiers in Group Dynamics' by Lewin. (Júly) Workshop at Gould Academy, Bethel. Establishment of National Training Laboratories.

References

Bales, R.F. (1950) *Personality and Interpersonal Behaviour*. New York:
   Holt Rinehart and Winston.
Barker, R., Dembo, T., and Lewin, K. (1941) Frustration and Regression:
   an Experiment with Young Children. *University of Iowa Studies in
   Child Welfare* 18 (1).
Belbin, R.M., Aston, B.R., and Mottram, R. (1976) Building Effective
   Management Teams. *Journal of General Management* 3 (3): 23-9.
Bennis, W.G. (1964) Patterns and Vicissitudes in T-Group Development.
   In L.P. Bradford, J.R. Gibb, and K.D. Benne (eds.), *T-Group Theory
   and Laboratory Method*. New York. John Wiley & Sons Inc.
Bion, W.R. (1968) *Experiences in Groups*. London: Tavistock
   Publications.
Bion, W.R. and Rickman, J. (1943) Intergroup Tensions in Therapy.
   Lancet. 27 November: 478-81.
Bradford, L.P., Gibb, J.R., and Benne, K.D. (1964) Two Educational
   Innovations. In L.P. Bradford, J.R. Gibb, and K.D. Benne (eds.),
   T-Group Theory and Laboratory Method. New York: John Wiley &
   Sons Inc.
Bunker, D.R. (1965) The Effect of Laboratory Education upon Individual
   Behaviour. In E.H. Schein and W.G. Bennis (eds.), *Personal and
   Organisational Change Through Group Methods*. New York: John
   Wiley & Sons Inc.

Campbell, J.P. and Dunnette, M.D. (1968) Effectiveness of T-Group
   Experiences in Managerial Training and Development. *Psychological
   Bulletin* 70 (2): 73-104.
Cartwright, D. and Zander, A. (1960) *Group Dynamics: Research and
   Theory*. London: Tavistock Publications.
Coch, L. and French, J.R.P. (1948) Overcoming Resistance to Change.
   Human Relations 1: 512-32.
Cooper, C.L. (1975) How Psychologically Dangerous are T-Groups and
   Encounter Groups? *Human Relations* 28 (3): 249-60.
Cooper, C.L. (1977), Taking the Terror out of T-Groups. *Personnel
   Management*. January 1977: 22-6.

Dicks, H.V. (1970) *Fifty Years of the Tavistock Clinic*. London: Routledge & Kegan Paul.

Emery, F.E. and Trist, E.L. (1969) Socio-technical Systems. In F.E. Emery (ed.), *Systems Thinking*. Harmondsworth: Penguin.

Fayol, H. (1949) *General and Industrial Management*. London: Pitman. (Translated by C. Storrs from the original *Administration Industrielle et Générale* 1916)
Ferenczi, S. (1916) *Contributions to Psychoanalysis*. Boston: Richard Badger.
Festinger, L. (1957) *A Theory of Cognitive Dissonance*. New York: Row Peterson.
Freud, S. (1951) *Beyond the Pleasure Principle*. Standard edition, Vol. 18. London: Hogarth Press.
Freud, S. (1951) *The Ego and the Id*. Standard edition, Vol. 19. London: Hogarth Press.
Freud, S. (1922) *Group Psychology and the Analysis of the Ego*. International Psycho-analytic Press.
Freud, S. (1974) *Introductory Lectures on Psychoanalysis*. Harmondsworth: Penguin Books.
Freud, S. (1951) *Totem and Taboo*. Standard edition, Vol. 13. London: Hogarth Press.

Haire, M. (1954) Group Dynamics in the Industrial Situation. In A. Kornhauser, R. Dubin, and A.M. Ross (eds.), *Industrial Conflict*. New York: McGraw Hill.
Hall, C.S. and Lindzey, G. (1968) The Relevance of Freudian Psychology and Related Viewpoints for the Social Sciences. In G. Lindzey and E. Aronson (eds.), *Handbook of Social Psychology*. Reading, Mass. Vol. 1. Addison-Wesley.
Herzberg, F., Mausner, B., and Snyderman, B.B. (1959) *The Motivation to Work*. New York: John Wiley & Sons Inc.
Higgin, G. and Bridger, H. (1965) *The Psychodynamics of an Intergroup Experience*. Tavistock pamphlet, No. 10. London.

Jaques, E. (1955) Social Systems as a Defence against Persecutory and Depressive Anxiety. In M. Klein, P. Heimann, and R. Money-Kyrle (eds.), *New directions in Psychoanalysis*. London: Tavistock Publications.
Jaques, E. (1951) *The Changing Culture of a Factory*. London: Tavistock Publications.
Jaques, E. (1970) A Contribution to a Discussion on Freud's 'Group Psychology and the Analysis of the Ego'. In E. Jaques, *Work, Creativity and Social Justice*. London: Heinemann.
Jaques, E. (1976) *A General Theory of Bureaucracy*. London: Heinemann.
Jones, E. (1948) Introduction. In M. Klein, *Contributions to Psychoanalysis 1921-1945*. London: Hogarth Press.

Katz, D. and Kahn, R.L. (1966) *The Social Psychology of Organisations.* New York: John Wiley & Sons Inc.

Klein, E.B. and Gould, L.J. (1973) Boundary Issues and Organisational Dynamics: a Case Study. *Social Psychiatry.* 8: 204-11.

Klein, M. (1946) Notes on some Schizoid Mechanisms. *International Journal of Psycho-analysis* 27: 99-110.

Klein, M. (1959) Our Adult World and its Roots in Infancy. *Human Relations* 12: 291-303. (Also published as Tavistock pamphlet No. 2. London: Tavistock Publications).

Klein, M., Heimann, P., and Money-Kyrle, R. (eds.) (1955) *New Directions in Psycho-analysis.* London: Tavistock Publications.

Lakin, M. (1972) *Interpersonal Encounter: Theory and Practice in Sensitivity Training.* New York: McGraw-Hill.

Le Bon, G. (1920) *The Crowd: a Study of the Popular Mind.* London: Fisher Unwin.

Lewin, K. (1952) Defining the Field at a Given Time. In D. Cartwright (ed.), *Field theory in social science.* London: Tavistock Publications.

Lewin, K. (1948) Experiments in Social Space. In G.W. Lewin (ed.), *Resolving Social Conflict.* New York. Harper and Bros.

Lewin, K. (1947) Frontiers in Group Dynamics. *Human Relations* 1 (1):

Lewin, K. (1972) Need, Force and Valence in Psychological Fields. In E.P. Hollander and R.G. Hunt (eds.), *Classic Contributions to Social Psychology.* London: Oxford University Press.

Lewin, K. (1936) *Principles of Topological Psychology.* New York: McGraw-Hill.

Lewin, K. (1952) Regression, Retrogression and Development. In D. Cartwright (ed.), *Field Theory in Social Science.* London: Tavistock Publications.

Lewin, K., Lippitt, R., and White, R.K. (1939) Patterns of Aggressive Behaviour in Experimentally Created 'Social Climates'. *International Journal of Social Psychology* 10: 271-99.

Lindzey, G. and Borgotta, E.F. (1954) Sociometric Measurement. In G. Lindzey (ed.), *Handbook of Social Psychology.* Reading, Mass: Addison Wesley.

Lippitt, R. (1949) *Training in Community Relations.* New York: Harper & Bros.

Maccoby, E.E., Newcomb, T.M., and Hartley, E.L. (1966) *Readings in Social Psychology.* London: Methuen.

Marrow, A.J. (1969) *The Practical Theorist: the Life and Work of Kurt Lewin.* New York: Basic Books Inc.

Maslow, A.H. (1970 *Motivation and Personality.* New York: Harper & Row.

Mayo, E. (1945) *The Social Problems of an Industrial Civilisation.* Cambridge, Mass: Harvard University Press.

McDougall, W. (1920) *The Group Mind.* Cambridge: Cambridge University Press.

Menzies, I.E.P. (1970) *The Functioning of Social Systems as a Defence against Anxiety*. Centre for Applied Social Research. London: Tavistock Institute of Human Relations.

Miller, E.J. (1975) Socio-Technical Systems in Weaving 1953-1970: A Follow-up Study. *Human Relations* 28 (4): 349-86.

Miller, E.J. and Gwynne, G.V. (1972) *A Life Apart*. London: Tavistock Publications.

Newcomb, T.M. (1966) Attitude Development as a Function of Reference Groups: the Bennington Study. In E.E. Maccoby, T.M. Newcomb, and E.L. Hartley (eds.), *Readings in Social Psychology*. London: Methuen.

Newcomb, T.M. (1943) *Personality and Social Changes*. New York: Dryden.

Parsons, H.M. (1974) What Happened at Hawthorne? *Science* 183: 922-32.

Pugh, D.S. (1966) Modern Organisation Theory. *Psychological Bulletin* 66 (4): 235-51.

Rice, A.K. (1969) Individual, Group and Intergroup Processes. *Human Relations* 22 (6): 565-84.

Rice, A.K. (1965) *Learning for Leadership*. London: Tavistock Publications.

Rice, A.K. (1958) *Productivity and Social Organisations: the Ahmedabad Experiment*. London: Tavistock Publications.

Rice, A.K. (1963) The Enterprise and its Environment. London: Tavistock Publications.

Rioch, M.J. (1970) The Work of Wilfred Bion on Groups. *Psychiatry* 33 (1): 56-66.

Roethlisberger, F.J., and Dickson, W.J. (1946) *Management and the Worker*. Cambridge, Mass: Harvard University Press.

Segal, H. (1973) *Introduction to the Work of Melanie Klein*. London: Hogarth Press.

Sherif, M. (1972) Experiments in Norm Formation. In E.P. Hollander and R.G. Hunt (eds.), *Classic Contributions to Social Psychology*. London: Oxford University Press.

Sherif, M. (1936) *The Psychology of Social Norms*. New York: Harper.

Smith, P.B. (1969) *Improving Skills in Working with People: the T-Group*. London: HMSO.

Sofer, C. (1972) *Organisations in Theory and Practice*. London: Heinemann.

Tavistock Institute of Human Relations. (1976) *Authority, Leadership and Organisation*. London: Tavistock.

Taylor, F.W. (1911) *Principles of Scientific Management*. New York: Harper.

Tiger, L. and Fox, R. (1972) *The Imperial Animal*. London: Secker & Warburg.

Trist, E.L. (1953) *Some Observations on the Machine Face as a Socio-Technical System*. A report to the Area General Manager, No. 1 Area, East Midlands Division (Report 341). London: Tavistock Institute of Human Relations.

Trist, E.L. and Bamforth, K.W. (1951) Some Social and Psychological Consequences of the Longwall Method of Coal-cutting. *Human Relations* 4 (1): 3-38.

Trist, E.L., Higgin, G.W., Murray, H. and Pollock, A.B. (1963) *Organisational Choice*. London: Tavistock Publications.

Trist, E.L. and Sofer, C. (1959) *Exploration in Group Relations*. Leicester: Leicester University Press.

Trotter, W. (1916) *Instincts of the Herd in Peace and War*. London: Fisher Unwin.

Turquet, P.M. (1974) Leadership: the Individual and the Group. In G.S. Gibbard, J.J. Hartman and R.D. Mann (eds.), *Analysis of Groups*. San Francisco: Jossey-Bass.

Turquet, P.M. (1975) Threats to Identity in the Large Group. In L. Kreeger (ed.), *The Large Group: Therapy and Dynamics*. London: Constable.

Von Bertalanffy, L. (1968) *General Systems Theory*. New York: George Brazillier.

Von Bertalanffy, L. (1969) The Theory of Open Systems in Physics and Biology. In F.E. Emery (ed.), *Systems Thinking*. Harmondsworth: Penguin.

Weber, W. (1930) *The Protestant Ethic and the Spirit of Capitalism*. London: Allen and Unwin.

Whitman, R.M. (1964) Psychodynamic Principles underlying T-Group Processes. In L.P. Bradford, J.R. Gibb, and K.D. Benne (eds.), *T-Group Theory and Laboratory Method*. New York: John Wiley & Sons Inc.

Name index

Subject index